Anonymous

Abstract of the Census of the Population

And other statistical Returns of Prince Edward Island, taken in the Year

1871

Anonymous

Abstract of the Census of the Population
And other statistical Returns of Prince Edward Island, taken in the Year 1871

ISBN/EAN: 9783337172978

Printed in Europe, USA, Canada, Australia, Japan

Cover: Foto ©ninafisch / pixelio.de

More available books at **www.hansebooks.com**

ABSTRACT

OF THE

CENSUS

OF

THE POPULATION,

AND OTHER

STATISTICAL RETURNS

OF

PRINCE EDWARD ISLAND,

TAKEN IN THE YEAR

1871.

Under the Act 33d Victoria, Cap. 6.

CHARLOTTETOWN:
REILLY & CO., PRINTERS, PRINCE STREET.
1871.

REPORT OF THE SUPERINTENDENT OF THE CENSUS RETURNS.

CHARLOTTETOWN,
August 23, 1871.

To the Clerk of the Executive Council:

SIR,—

The results of the Census of Prince Edward Island, taken in the month of April of the present year, are now, after a careful compilation and final revision of all the statistical returns, respectfully submitted for the information of Her Majesty's Government.

The series of prepared tables herewith transmitted, contain an abstract and classification of the details to be found in the accompanying 241 books, as filled in and returned by the 69 enumerators employed in that service.

On the 18th of May last, I had the honor of addressing to His Honor the Lieutenant Governor in Council, a brief preliminary report, or a rough grand total of the population and of the religious denominations, as these appeared on the face of the returns, and before the figures were finally checked and tested—which total approximated very closely to that now exhibited.

The defective state of several of the returns necessitated a longer delay than I had anticipated in the completion of this task ; and although I was not able to adopt the novel expedient of the Registrar General of Victoria, Australia, who, desirous of making the recent taking of the census of that great Province a thorough success, offered a reward of a half sovereign to every householder who could shew that his household had been overlooked by the enumerator ; nor yet favored, like the same high official in London, with confidential returns in sealed envelopes, of the ages of ladies whom no persuasion nor threats could induce to disclose their years to the enumerator, because of their personal acquaintance with the latter functionary ; although possessing—I repeat—none of these advantages, still I believe that several important omissions have been supplied, and corrections made, as the result of the newspaper advertisements and circular letters to which I had recourse, in order to attain the desired accuracy and completeness of these returns. The last of these circulars to which I expect a response, having been answered yesterday, I have now, with the efficient aid of my temporary assistant, brought this duty to a close, although in its progress I have been obliged to remove my last retreat in this Colonial Building is without the least privacy or seclusion, open to all-comers, and especially so to enterprizing "interviewers" of the press—tho whole affording an example of "the pursuit of knowledge under difficulties" exceedingly discouraging, and seldom experienced, it is to be hoped, in similar situations.

The value and importance of a correct and reliable census cannot be over estimated, when it is considered that the intention is to ascertain the increase which has taken place in the wealth and resources of the Colony, in its trade and manufactures, and in the productions, especially of its agriculture and fisheries. The undertaking being of the highest importance to the country, and of great interest to each inhabitant, it should have been carefully and accurately performed, and every facility and assistance given to the enumerators in their interesting work ; yet it is certain that in some instances the necessary information was withheld, or only partially supplied. The taking of the Census is a process for the success of which it is necessary to obtain the general and cordial co-operation of the people. A penalty may nominally be threatened, but practically, it is never enforced. To give a few instances: in the returns from one Township the remark is made: "Several on this road appeared unwilling to give a full return of statistics, owing to an erroneous impression that the end in view was to impose a tax to meet the expenditure of the railroad." In another Township a householder is represented as "a very great miser, very unwilling to give statistics I verily believe he had over 600 bushels of oats; he, however, gave in but three hundred bushels." In other cases in the same district, the quantity of butter produced is not returned, with the remark, " cannot tell how much—they ate it all." In another instance the proprietor of well known cloth mills is represented as refusing to give any information whatever, relative to his factory or its products, but instead, hurled anathemas at the head of the enumerator and his employers. Whether this person has been brought to a better frame of mind by a prosecution at the instance of the proper officer, does not appear.

On a comparative view of the present and the last census, discrepancies appear in connection with our fisheries. "Boats owned for fishing purposes" are set down at 1183, while the number to man them is but 1646 ; and in four different districts the boats exceed the men in number. Again, the " fishing establishments" have doubled in ten years, while the number of men employed is 672 fewer. This may be in part explained by giving all the boats owned by all the individuals combining the occupations of farmer and fisherman, but enumerating in most cases tho " men" engaged in fishing, under the category of *farmers*, alone, except of course in the regular fishing establishments.* So, also, in minor details of the population, as well as in some important farming productions, a decrease is shown where a considerable increase should have appeared. The tabular statements will show these more succinctly.

* While going through the press, additional information has been received, marked APPENDIX, explaining that farmers owning boats have not been put down as " men engaged in fishing," hence the disparity between "men" and boats above referred to.

The "General Remarks" appended are given, for the most part, in the words of the returs or slightly abridged to avoid iteration; an exception occurs in one of the Townships where the officer employed intersperses amid his descriptions of the state of the roads, and the aspect of the farms, &c., some lively biographical sketches of certain of the inhabitants of his District, which, although probably possessing some interest to the future local chronicler of "Hardscrabble" and regions adjoining, can have no appreciable value as elements in our public records or Colonial statistics. On this head, a few illustrations may suffice as "curiosities of the Census:"

One settler is described as "a very slack fellow; works at Brickmaking in Summer." A second as "a very poor man—too many small children, including twins." Another, again, "a very greedy man, in rather poor circumstances, raised a large useless family." Also, " two old maids, very nervous about taxation, very well-to do." Another, "a mechanic of a very indifferent kind, came here thirty years ago, a mere pauper, but who is now immensely rich. His daughters dress in nothing less than black silk at the present time." And lastly, another is described as "a man who is death on railroads and railroad men."

Of these extracts, it may be observed, that it has always been conceded that a large family brought up to habits of industry is the poor man's best fortune in the woods of America, as well as the most valuable acquisition to the State. The instance of the "indifferent" mechanic proves the value of this country as a home for the poorest immigrant—both skilled and unskilled labor being sure of meeting with ample encouragement and reward ; while in the case of the hostile anti-railroad man, it need only be said that should he not happily be diverted from his destructive purposes, then he who first gave due warning of danger cannot be held answerable for the possible consequences.

In summarizing the contents of these tables, the primary fact to be noticed is the increase of the population since the last numbering in 1861, when it stood at 80,857. The total population of Prince Edward Island in April, 1871, is 94,021, including 323 Micmac Indians; decennial increase, 13,164, or 16.28 per cent. Total number of males, 47,121; total females, 46,900; excess of males, 221; number of families, 14,841; average number to each family, 6.34.

Religious denominations, viz:—Church of England, 7,220; Presbyterian Church of Lower Provinces, 18,603; Church of Scotland, 10,976; total Presbyterians, 29,579; Roman Catholics, 40,765; Methodists, 8,361; Baptists, 4,371; Bible Christians, 2,709; Quakers, 8; Universalists, 77; other denominations, 931.

Total number of children between the ages of 5 and 16, 25,952; males from 21 to 45, 12,790; males from 21 to 60, 17,558; births in the past year, 2,344; deaths, 941; natives of the Island, 80,271; natives of other countries, 13,750; deaf and dumb, 70; blind, 64; insane, 188.

Principal productions of the soil raised last year:—

Bushels Wheat,	269,392
(1447 bus. being winter Wheat)	
" Barley,	176,441
" Oats,	3,128,576
" Potatoes,	3,375,726
" Turnips,	395,358
Tons of Hay,	68,349
Pounds of Flax,	27,282
Mowing Machines,	1,024
Stumping do.,	133
Haymaking do.,	578
Hay Elevators,	115
Mud Diggers,	1,402
Threshing Machines,	1,607
Number of yards of fulled Cloth manufactured last year,	150,975
Ditto not fulled,	428,313
Number of Horses,	25,329
Neat Cattle,	62,984
Sheep,	147,364
Hogs,	52,514
Brewing & Distilling Establishments,	11
Tanneries,	58
Grist Mills,	145
Carding Mills,	47
Saw Mills,	181
Fulling and Dressing Mills,	13
Cloth factories,	4
Churches,	187
Schoolhouses,	343
Number of Fishing Establishments,	176
Barrels of Mackerel cured last year,	16,047
Ditto Herring or Alewives,	16,831
Quintals of Codfish or Hake,	15,649
Pounds of Hake Sounds cured last year,	12,522
Gallons of Fish Oil made last year,	11,662
Quantity of preserved Shell and other Fish prepared last year, (lbs.)	6,711
Salmon taken last year, (value)	£368 10s. 0d.
Number of Fish Barrels manufactured last year,	42,278
Number of Coopers' Shops,	65
Number of Boats owned for fishing purposes,	1,183
Number of men engaged in fishing,	1,646

LAND AND PRODUCE, VIZ:

Number of acres held in fee simple,	697,598
Increase since 1861,	241,655
Number of acres held by lease, or agreement for lease,	279,601
Decrease,	127,568
Number of acres held by verbal agreement,	20,931
Decrease,	17,509
No. of acres held by occupants being neither freeholders nor leaseholders,	30,110
Decrease,	34,526
Number of acres of arable land held by all families,	445,103
Increase,	76,975
Wheat raised. decrease in bushels since 1861,	78,180
Barley, do ,	46,754
Oats, increase, do.,	909,998
*Potatoes, increase, do.,	803,391
Turnips, increase, do.,	46,574
Buckwheat raised last year, bush.,	75,109
Do., increase, do.,	24,982
Clover Seed, bush ,	3,219
Timothy Seed, do.,	8,645
Hay, increase in tons,	37,260
Lime Kilns, increase,	68
Brick Kilns, do ,	11

*A typographical error in some uncorrected copies of the last census, of 400,000 bushels of potatoes in excess, leaves the true increase this year at 803,391 bushels. In the number of hogs in the same census, a like error occurs—the real total then being 38,553, giving an increase, as above, of 13,961.

Mackerel, barrels of, increase,	8,884
Herring and Alewives, decrease,	5,584
Codfish, quintals, decrease,	24,126
Fish Oil, decrease in gallons,	5,947
Cheese, increase in lbs.,	46,290
Butter, do.,	270,454
Fulled Cloth, increase in yards,	28,035
Not fulled, do.,	124,636
Horses, increase,	6,564
Neat Cattle, do.,	2,972
Sheep, do.,	40,119
Hogs, do.,	13,961
Churches, increase,	31
Schoolhouses, do.,	41
Threshing Machines, do.,	751

Products and articles not enumerated in the Census of 1861, viz:—

Bushels Beans raised last year,	584
Bush. Peas, do.,	741
Bush. Vetches, do.,	32½
Pounds Flax, do.,	27,282
Sewing Machines,	644
Pianos, Melodeons and Organs,	479

From the foregoing summary it will be seen that Agriculture is the largest interest of the Colony, involving more than any other branch of industry, the labor, the wealth, and the welfare of the people; and the facts furnished each decade by the Census, concern alike producers and consumers, mechanics and all engaged in commerce. This is the great material interest of the country by which all others thrive, and which has the right to demand the constant and chief regard of the Legislature.

The schedules of the next census—the enumerators being first most carefully selected— should embrace with entire accuracy all the conditions, proceeds and results of the industry of the country at large. The materials gathered in this numbering, despite the imperfections pointed out, afford a good basis for future comparison. And if the future of Prince Edward Island, in view of the intelligence and energy of her farmers, her public free schools, her agricultural associations, her free press, and the expanding and humanizing influences of her institutions, shall continue to exhibit the same steady progress which we find in the past, then the results of each succeeding census, dry and uninteresting as they may seem to those who see in them but mere columns of figures, may teach lessons not simply of political economy, but of daily duty, the benefits of which shall be reaped alike by the present and future generations. And encouraged by the fact that inventive genius and mechanical skill are rapidly introducing improved machinery, overcoming the chief difficulty of the farmer in the high price and scarcity of labor, there are those now living who may witness the productions of our soil trebled and quadrupled, affording abundant wholesome food and healthy employment to teeming thousands in this Garden of the Gulf, which has been given to man to dress and to keep it.

JOHN McNEILL,
Supt. of Census Returns.

Note.—In the following tables appear three separate columns—following the Schedule in the Act—for the quantity " of cloth manufactured " last year; the *last* of these is superfluous and unreliable; the *first two* columns devoted respectively to the number of yards of cloth "fulled" and "not fulled," contain the total of these articles.

Grand Total—Abstract of the Population Returns of P. E. Island—1871.

MALES						FEMALES						Deaf and Dumb	Blind	No. not Vaccinated, nor had Small Pox	Married	Single	Insane	Married last year	Deaths last year	Births last year	Total number	Males	Females	Members of the Church of England	Freebyterian church of lower Provinces	Kirk of Scotland	Roman Catholics	Methodists	Baptists	Bible Christians	Quakers	Universalists	Other Denominations	NATIVES OF					INDIANS INCLUDED					
Under 5 years	From 5 to 10	From 10 to 21	From 21 to 45	From 45 to 60	Upwards of 60	Under 5 years	From 5 to 16	From 16 to 21	From 21 to 45	From 45 to 60	Upwards of 60																							England	Scotland	Ireland	British Provinces	Prince Edward Island	Other countries	Total No. of Males	Total No. of Females	No. of families	Population in 1871	Population in 1855	Population in 1861	Increase since 1861	Decrease since 1861
7568	13279	5633	12780	4768	2952	7188	12673	3672	4422	2439	70	64	46349	26320	67818	188	650	941	2344	98698	151	112	7290	18903	10916	40442	8361	4371	2709	8	77	931	1957	4128	8112	3946	80271	364	41121	46390	14841	94021	62599	71496	80857	18319	55

Grand Total—Abstract of Statistical Returns of P. E. Island, 1871.

No. of persons holding Land of				No. Acres held					Produce raised during the past Year.																			
First quality	Second quality	Third quality	In fee simple	By lease or agreement for lease	By verbal agreement	As occupants being neither freeholders nor leaseholders	No. of Acres of arable land	Bushels of wheat	Bushels of winter wheat	Bushels of barley	Bushels of oats	Bushels of buckwheat	Bushels of Indian corn	Bushels of clover seed	Bushels of timothy seed	Bushels of potatoes	Bushels of turnips	Bushels of other roots	Apples and other fruit, (value)	Tons of hay	Bushels of beans	Bushels of peas	Bushels of vetches	Pounds of flax	No. of flax manufactories	No. of acres covered with shell manure	No. of acres covered with lime	Pounds of cheese made last year	Pounds of butter made last year	No. of fanning mills	No. of mowing machines	No. of stumping machines	No. of hay-making machines	No. of hay elevators	No. of mud diggers	No. of other useful machines	No. of carts, trucks, & truck-waggons	No. of riding-waggons and carriages, wood-sleds and jaunting sleighs	No. of yards of fulled cloth manufactured last year	do. and fulled	No. of threshing machines	No. of horses	No. of neat cattle	No. of sheep
3894	6125	1403	69160	27060	29931	30110	415103	207913	1147	176141	3129570	75109	2411	5219	8645	3375726	205557	59923	£3141 1s	68319	581	7413	325	21283	8	32952	15119	156521	981939	1292	1024	137	518	113	1402	2500	11205	24881	159975	428313	1601	25320	62984	147964

Grand Total—Abstract of Statistical Returns of P. E. Island, 1871.

No. of hogs	No. of churches	No. of school houses	No. of brewing and distilling establishments.	No. of tanneries	Pounds of leather manufactured last year	Pounds of tobacco manufactured last year	No. of fishing establishments	No. of barrels of mackerel cured last year	do. Herrings or Alewives, do.	No. of quintals of cod fish or hake cured last year	No. of boats owned for fishing purposes	Gallons of fish oil made last year	No. of men engaged in fishing	Pounds of fish barrels manufactured last year	No. of cooper's shops	Pounds of hake sounds cured last year	Quantity of preserved shell and other fish prepared last year	Salmon taken last year, (value)	No. of grist mills	No. of saw mills.	MILLS, whether driven by water steam or horse power.		
																					No. of fulling and dressing mills	Number of shingle and lath mills	No. of steam engines for mechanical and other purposes	No. of barrels of lime last year	No. of brick kilns	No. of bricks manufactured last year	No. of carriages and sleighs manufactured last year	No. of cloth factories	No. of sewing machines	No. of pianos, melodeons, and organs
52514	187	343	11	58	197031	69359	176	16047	16831	15649	1183	11662	1646	42278	65	12522	6711 lbs	368 10	145	181	13	130	12	116	56737	20	1556245	1207	4	644	479

Abstract of the Returns of the Population of P. E. Island, 1871.

ELECTORAL DISTRICTS, &c.	Number of Families	MALES						FEMALES						Deaf and Dumb	Blind	Not vaccinated nor had Small Pox.	Married	Single	Insane	Married during the past year	Deaths during the past year	Births during the past year	Total No. in each family, including servants and apprentices	INDIANS	
		Under 5 years	From 5 to 16	From 16 to 21	From 21 to 45	From 45 to 60	Upwards of 60	Under 5 years	From 5 to 16	From 16 to 21	From 21 to 45	From 45 to 60	Upwards of 60											Males	Females
PRINCE COUNTY.																									
First District,	1281	821	1169	476	1189	366	295	777	1105	510	1114	295	164	9	1	5440	2459	5732	22	18	71	192	8191	7	15
Second District,	717	423	688	260	696	179	123	420	640	287	636	150	85	1		3200	1226	3353	6	17	39	146	4579	78	78
Third District,	822	488	765	293	694	215	171	443	737	314	756	242	125	9	2	4042	1574	3729	12	28	58	182	5303	22	13
Fourth District,	1048	559	888	329	860	297	232	574	905	378	935	271	182	3	1	2273	2074	4356	7	37	68	176	6430	13	18
Fifth District,	542	339	464	183	525	190	71	298	521	253	539	117	61	1	3	1390	1032	2529	4	11	31	120	3561	1	
Total,	4410	2630	3974	1541	3974	1307	802	2512	3908	1742	3982	1075	617	23	7	16351	8365	19699	51	111	267	816	28064	114	124
KING'S COUNTY.																									
First District,	964	370	766	316	845	306	191	327	672	354	899	281	183	2	8	1667	1578	3932	12	36	56	89	5510	2	12
Second District,	845	365	760	299	728	285	185	358	651	384	806	366	146	4	4	2368	1328	3861	10	18	32	118	5189		
Third District,	845	432	873	319	754	259	184	380	742	354	801	259	149	6	15	2306	1444	4062	11	32	73	146	5506		
Fourth District,	806	480	862	379	714	310	183	452	792	396	786	365	140	4	7	2975	1661	4138	13	37	59	150	5799	2	2
G. Town & Royalty,	200	69	135	67	159	50	36	58	154	83	168	48	29	1		207	277	779	3	5	47		1056		
Total,	3660	1716	3402	1380	3200	1210	779	1575	3011	1521	3460	1159	647	16	35	9523	6288	16772	46	178	225	520	23060	4	4
QUEEN'S COUNTY.																									
First District,	1438	748	1354	513	1218	420	301	751	1220	570	1291	422	239	9	9	5571	2509	5538	7	35	106	213	9047		
Second District,	1331	660	1163	569	1121	462	276	649	1154	624	1106	454	222	14	6	3961	2418	6042	15	48	83	209	8460	15	20
Third District,	1212	611	1113	517	1058	472	269	527	1102	580	1101	404	232	2	1	3815	2206	5177	3	45	50	175	7983	12	16
Fourth District,	1264	625	1104	473	1040	427	300	590	1115	600	1221	426	290	5	6	4659	2233	6044	13	77	76	206	8277	6	8
Ch. Town & Royalty	1526	558	1109	640	1176	470	225	584	1163	697	1511	482	192	2		2069	2301	6506	53	56	134	205	8807		
Total,	6771	3202	5903	2712	5616	2251	1371	3101	5754	3071	6230	2188	1175	31	22	20075	11607	30907	91	263	449	1008	42574	33	44
Total, P. E. Island	14841	7548	13279	5633	12790	4768	2952	7188	12673	6334	13672	4422	2439	70	64	45949	26320	67378	188	550	941	2344	93698	151	172

Grand Total—Abstract of the Population Returns of P. E. Island—1871.

ELECTORAL DISTRICTS, &c.	Members of the Church of England	Presbyterian church of lower Provinces	Kirk of Scotland	Roman Catholics	Methodists	Baptists	Bible Christians	Quakers	Universalists	Other Denominations	NATIVES OF England	NATIVES OF Scotland	NATIVES OF Ireland	NATIVES OF British Provinces	NATIVES OF Prince Edward Island	NATIVES OF Other countries	Total No. of Males	Total No. of Females	Population in 1871	Population in 1848	Population in 1855	Population in 1861	Increase since 1861	Decrease since 1861
Prince County.																								
First District,	568	1296	90	5502	433	59	127	2	4	10	110	76	215	393	7383	14	4233	3980	8213	2943	4164	5419	2794	
Second District,	589	1300	71	1363	374	95	718	1		68	142	77	100	132	4120	8	2432	2298	4730	1988	2443	3205	1525	
Third District,	286	1364	95	3255	170	88	25	1	1	19	42	67	64	120	5003	7	2708	2630	5338	3640	4071	4690	648	
Fourth District,	232	1121	680	2007	1561	657	12	1	10	149	166	142	362	161	5585	14	3196	3263	6459	5202	5363	6039	420	
Fifth District,	767	658	123	1340	349	143	14	2	25	140	94	56	62	241	3078	30	1773	1789	3562	1224	1511	2048	1514	
Total,	2442	5739	1059	13467	2887	1042	896	6	40	386	554	418	803	1047	25169	73	14342	13960	28302	15017	17552	21401	6901	
King's County.																								
First District,	56	444	22	4502	31	410	1			44	30	129	108	164	5042	37	2796	2718	5514	4340	4716	5099	415	
Second District,	192	1401	74	3383	50	65	19			5	48	172	195	183	4563	28	2626	2561	5187	3883	4098	4734	455	
Third District,	164	789	896	2862	207	495	61			45	106	411	254	196	4527	12	2821	2685	5506	3226	3853	4495	1011	
Fourth District,	147	2513	624	1088	426	263	572		9	162	121	625	148	248	4636	21	2930	2873	5803	3348	3937	4772	1031	
G'Town & Royalty,	156	52	272	547	10	5	3			11	15	44	41	179	772	5	516	540	1056	678	768	831	225	
Total,	712	5199	1878	12371	724	1238	656		9	267	320	1381	746	970	19540	103	11691	11377	23066	15475	17342	19931	3137	
Queen's County.																								
First District,	990	3416	1060	2243	913	313	20	1	1	60	156	794	524	120	7425	19	4554	4493	9047	8430	7765	8233	814	
Second District,	870	1580	1448	2720	605	776	309			62	269	391	210	80	7499	11	4266	4229	8495	7090	7886	8550		55
Third District,	321	756	1087	4188	911	415	326			29	194	181	532	98	6971	7	4049	3962	8011	6680	7236	7830	181	
Fourth District,	278	1384	3391	2119	440	331	230		22	82	54	717	241	177	7070	18	4041	4250	8291	7190	7702	8206	85	
Ch'Town & Royalty,	1507	499	1103	3328	1791	256	272	1	5	45	410	246	656	745	6597	153	4178	4629	8807	4717	6613	6706	2101	
Total,	3966	7665	8039	14598	1750	2091	1157	2	28	278	1083	2329	2163	1229	35562	208	21088	21563	42651	32101	36602	39525	3181	55
Total, P. E. Island	7220	18603	10976	40442	5361	4371	2709	8	77	931	1957	4128	3712	3246	80271	384	47121	46900	94021	62599	71496	80857	13219	55

Abstract of the Statistical Returns of P. E. Island, 1871.

ELECTORAL DISTRICTS, &c.	No. of persons holding Land of			No. of acres held				No. of acres of arable Land.	PRODUCE RAISED DURING THE PAST YEAR.									
	First quality	Second quality	Third quality	In fee simple	By lease or agreement for lease	By verbal agreement	As occupants, being neither freeholders nor leaseholders		Bushels of Wheat	Bushels of Winter Wheat	Bushels of Barley	Bushels of Oats	Bushels of Buckwheat	Bushels of Indian Corn	Bushels of Clover Seed	Bushels of Timothy Seed	Bushels of Potatoes	Bushels of Turnips
PRINCE COUNTY.																		
First District.	445	545	114	80603	18586	683	208	51701	33778	159	7052	172063	6803	3491	154	428	319041	17303
Second District,	314	241	49	36236	26412	4534	946	22762	18708	58	4222	101005	5849	50	114	447	139486	9749
Third District,	196	363	191	48522	14557	679	916	25208	16915	172	16680	150255	6110	1555	137	611	187585	19993
Fourth District,	323	430	70	62056	27634	403	1252	39067	20903	—	13823	366332	17526	114	304	1215	202384	20291
Fifth District,	98	43	5	16361	2721	80	—	7533	5132	150	4172	56622	3471	95	85	186	70421	7128
Total,	1376	1622	429	233788	84912	6379	3322	146371	95436	539	45999	855277	39259	2601	795	2888	1008017	83464
KING'S COUNTY.																		
First District,	449	320	23	55062	8659	1780	6912	21595	11369	87	17527	188197	847	71	12	378	183529	5642
Second District,	138	540	142	53781	4652	6387	7689	21859	13803	54	12217	164244	2354	146	14	416	188581	9409
Third District,	223	501	73	73128	2071	166	1505	25193	7711	80	7932	179489	2679	7	21	397	245929	6879
Fourth District,	143	564	141	49694	10485	916	4170	21930	12806	61	6495	150396	2185	8	813	282	213130	6155
Geo'town & Royalty	62	24	13	5118	204	290	—	2195	973	—	460	10582	70	3	2	14	22934	1073
Total,	1015	1949	392	237583	26070	9589	20276	92772	46662	2334	44631	692854	7635	235	70	1488	854053	32158
QUEEN'S COUNTY.																		
First District,	254	864	184	45673	58961	923	5270	49852	29969	50	19163	377603	16759	24	19564	1074	348935	34903
Second District,	583	484	38	47052	41933	1971	657	50135	42945	102	26909	411393	6101	50	1044	975	440449	74757
Third District,	263	585	207	39678	59061	1573	100	52610	2914	164	23533	404426	2925	20	202	954	354082	76934
Fourth District,	352	605	234	93681	8599	540	485	46831	21903	—	9737	354925	2207	21	88	1186	392298	34674
Ch'town & Royalty,	51	16	9	143	65	6	—	5832	1943	359	6469	28094	328	—	3	79	27092	58378
Total,	1503	2554	672	226227	168610	5013	6512	205160	125847	675	85811	1580441	2821	115	2354	4268	1512756	278736
Total, P. E. Island	3894	6125	1493	697598	279601	20081	30110	445103	267945	14474	170441	3128576	75109	2411	3219	8645	3375726	395358
Total, as per census 1861,	4073	5180	1488	455942	107169	38440	64636	368127	346125	—	2231954	2218578	50127	—	322	—	2572885	348784
Increase,	—	945	5	2416552	—	—	—	76975	—	—	909998	21082	—	2897	—	803391	46574		
Decrease,	179	—	—	—	127568	17500	34526	—	78180	—	46754	—	—	—	—	—		

NOTE.—In the columns where "increase" and "decrease" both appear blank, no returns were made under these heads in the Census of former years.

Abstract of the Statistical Returns of P. E. Island, 1871, (*continued.*)

ELECTORAL DISTRICTS, &c.	Produce raised during the past Year. Bushels of other Roots	Apples and other Fruit, (value) £	s.	d.	Tons of Hay	Bushels of Beans	Bushels of Peas	Bushels of Vetches	Pounds of Flax.	No. of Flax Manufactories	No. of acres covered with shell Manure	No. of acres covered with Lime	Pounds of Cheese manufactured during the past year	Pounds of Butter manufactured during the past year	No. of Fanning Mills	No. of Mowing Machines	No. of Stumping Machines	No. of Hay-making Machines	No. of Hay Elevators	No. of Mud Diggers
PRINCE COUNTY.																				
First District,	6	£ 52	18	0	2742	19½	58½	1	1472	1	2324½	—	1220	58904	70	28	5	29	8	101
Second District,	246½	133	14	0	3210	74	86½	1	1109	1	997	267	3371	52779	49	17	—	6	1	62
Third District,	21	64	10	0	4622	27½	113¾	—	2847	—	3067	173	8494	53231	109	53	15	15	17	131
Fourth District,	90	490	9	0	7480	29	36		637	—	4886	1166	9302	126403	237	160	18	19	28	157
Fifth District,	20	7	0	0	2209	10½	31	—	427	—	1108	184	350	22275	49	39	3	8	10	41
Total, - -	383½	748	11	0	20263	160½	325½	2½	6492	2	12382½	1789	22737	313692	614	297	36	77	59	492
KING'S COUNTY,																				
First District,	38	£ 112	16	0	3154	25½	7	—	5301	—	88	17	21363	53819	75	22	2	46	—	25
Second District,	239½	134	14	6	2386	104	52	8	1904	—	157	4	14018	60042	62	41	8	22	—	13
Third District,	46	61	2	0	6686	86	81	—	2802½	—	486½	234	7022	41916	50	35	8	28	1	43
Fourth District,	113	292	4	0	2490	37½	44	—	1296	1	246	398	4781	33617	44	30	5	19	—	46
Geo'town & Royalty	170	97	10	0	382	42½	18	—	60	—	94	20	679	4614	11	1	—	—	—	6
Total, - -	612½	698	6	6	15098	295½	152½	8	11453	1	1071½	673½	47893	194007	242	129	23	115	1	133
QUEEN'S COUNTY.																				
First District,	216½	£ 205	7	0	7286	44	20½	—	1802	—	6523	1105½	11833	108946	228	94	18	36	25	183
Second District.	199	285	17	0	10697	3	101	22	877	—	10029	4115½	30309	138788	233	172	27	51	15	315
Third District.	120	799	0	0	7448	28	71	1	998	—	2326	6494	21551	114854	257	192	22	190	4	186
Fourth District,	272	404	0	0	6111	48	71	—	6656	5	1174	519	20798	99482	98	111	5	97	4	72
Ch'town & Royalty	1183	90	0	0	1602	5	—	—	3	—	446	1022	405	12270	25	29	2	12	7	21
Total, - -	1990½	1784	4	0	32988	128	263½	22	9336½	6	19498	13256	84894	474340	830	598	74	386	55	777
Total P. E. Island,	2992½	3141	1	6	68349½	584½	741½	32½	27282	9	32952	15719	155524	981039	1692	1024	133	578	115	1402
Total as per census, 1861,	—	—			81088½	—	—	—	—	—	—	—	109233½	711485	—	—	—	—	—	—
Increase,	—	—			872601½	—	—	—	—	—	—	—	46290½	270454	—	—	—	—	—	—
Decrease,	—	—			—	—	—	—	—	—	—	—	—	—	—	—	—	—	—	—

NOTE.—In the columns where "increase" and "decrease both appear blank, no returns were made under these heads in the Census of former years.

Abstract of Statistical Returns of P. E. Island, 1871. (continued.)

ELECTORAL DISTRICTS, &c.	No. of other useful machines	No. of Carts, Trucks and Truck wagons	No. of Riding Wagons & Carriages, Woodsleds & Jaunting Sleighs	No. of yards of Cloth manufactured during the past year (fulled)	Do. (not fulled)	No. of Threshing Machines	No. of Horses	No. of Neat Cattle	No. of Sheep	No. of Hogs	No. of Churches	No. of Schoolhouses	No. of Brewing and Distilling Establishments	No. of Vineries	Pounds of Leather manufactured during the past year	Pounds of Tobacco manufactured during the past year	No. of Fishing Establishments	Barrels of Mackerel cured during the past year	Barrels of Herrings or Alewives cured during the past year	Quintals of Codfish or Hake cured during the past year	No. of Boats owned for fishing purposes
PRINCE COUNTY.																					
First District,	32	1155	1936	11875	45173	68	2169	4827	19617	4478	8	22		6	4400		7	76	6909	5575	5913	385
Second District,	303	579	1158	7604	24181	74	1452	3553	6564	2513	19	23		1	1542			4	23	2034	668	70
Third District,	56	857	1730	12447	21271	73	1616	4064	8993	3284	7	20		1	1372			5	215	2665	623	67
Fourth District,	101	1453	2608	13356	33145	266	2472	6251	15160	3826	16	24	1	4	6914			1	3	105	15	14
Fifth District,	406	384	796	2597	10712	38	562	1152	2779	1162	8	10	2	3	10000	7500					
Total,	898	4428	8228	47879	134482	519	8271	19847	46104	15263	55	99	3	15	24229	7507	88	1150	10379	7119	536
KING'S COUNTY.																					
First District,	5	928	1546	8662	25574	96	1527	4635	8501	4252	8	23			873		39	2811	6334	4586	222
Second District,	23	843	1485	7868	17385	94	1467	4064	8261	4100	8	25	1	3	2750		5	877	424	799	79
Third District,	4	815	1026	10218	69783	57	1354	3821	8060	2679	17	21	3	5300			6	82	159	108	31
Fourth District,	75	828	1135	9521	23683	56	1195	3628	9013	2317	11	24	1	4	185		3	1264	195	550	60
Geo'town & Royalty	5	119	177	855	2537	4	125	300	585	248	3	2	1	2	1800		7	731	136	315	20
Total,	112	3533	5369	37124	138962	307	5668	16448	34420	13596	47	93	3	12	10908		60	46274	1547	6358	412
QUEEN'S COUNTY.																					
First District,	419	1348	2945	16852	45292	179	2860	6574	16484	5904	19	37		6	6355		6	6284	1323	389	56
Second District,	676	1525	2732	17537	39690	230	2886	6634	16857	5686	22	38		1	600		9	6144	429	138	25
Third District,	66	1633	2454	16340	26195	250	2576	6136	15526	6529	17	28		5	10800		7	717	1180	448	43
Fourth District,	94	1480	2352	15013	43987	106	2438	6509	17205	4615	18	38		7	6339		3	60	1512	4474	91
Ch'town & Royalty,	244	318	804	230	305	16	630	842	768	921	9	10	5	12	137800	61892	5	2250	460	750	20
Total,	1499	6331	11287	65972	154869	781	11390	26689	66840	23655	85	151	5	31	161894	61892	30	42704	4904	21724	235
Total P. E. Island,	2509	14295	24884	150975	428313	1607	25329	62984	147364	52514	187	343	11	58	197091	69399	178	160474	16831	15649	3183
Total as per census, 1861,				122940	303676	856	18765	60012	107245	38558	150	302	20	55	143803		89	7163	22416	38776	1239
Increase,				28035	124636	751	6561	2972	40119	13961	31	41		3	53228		87	8884			56
Decrease,													9						5584	24126	

NOTE.—In the columns where "Increase" and "decrease" both appear blank, no returns were made under these heads in the Census of former years.

Abstract of Statistical Returns of P. E. Island, 1871. concluded.)

ELECTORAL DISTRICTS, &c.	Gallons of Fish Oil made during the past year	No. of Men engaged in fishing	No. of Fish Barrels manufactured during the past year	No. of Coopers' Shops	Pounds of Hake Sounds cured during the past year	Quantity of preserved Shell and other Fish prepared during the past year	Salmon taken during the past year (value)	Mills, whether driven by water, steam or horse power.					No. of Lime Kilns	Barrels of Lime manufactured during the past year	No. of Brick Kilns	No. of Bricks manufactured during the past year	No. of Carriages and Sleighs manufactured during the past year	Yards of Cloth manufactured during the past year	No. of Cloth Factories	No. of Sewing Machines	No. of Pianos, Melodeons and Organs
								No. of Grist Mills	No. of Carding Mills	No. of Saw Mills	No. of Fulling and Dressing Mills	No. of Shingle and Lath Mills	No. of Steam Engines for mechanical and other purposes									
PRINCE COUNTY.							lbs.															
First District,	3858	660	29762	14	4003	—	£ 150 0 0	12	3	16	2	9	—	—	—	1	90000	166	45519	—	13	12
Second District,	257	49	1275	5	—	—	—	8	4	15	—	7	—	1	300	—	—	22	25794	—	8	2
Third District,	388	18	—	—	311	—	—	6	2	8	—	5	2	4	810	2	3700	11	33184	1	13	2
Fourth District,	8	4	—	1	—	—	—	13	5	14	1	14	—	13	4200	—	—	195	29278	—	59	19
Fifth District,	—	—	—	—	—	—	—	2	1	1	—	1	1	3	2200	—	—	107	—	—	66	34
Total,	4511	731	31037	20	4003	311	£ 150 0 0	41	15	54	3	36	3	21	7510	3	93700	491	133835	1	159	69
KING'S COUNTY.																						
First District,	3045	132	3710	4	6382	—	—	12	4	12	2	12	—	2	400	—	—	34	19903	—	6	7
Second District,	376	80	250	1	6	—	118 5 0	11	3	11	1	15	—	1	100	1	60000	32	11177	2	7	2
Third District,	74	19	—	—	—	—	—	8	4	18	2	15	—	8	762	—	—	31	9420	—	11	4
Fourth District,	1743	107	390	8	1975	5000	—	8	1	16	—	9	—	17	3466	—	—	78	20708	—	4	—
Geo'town & Royalty	197	67	790	3	6	—	—	—	—	—	—	—	—	1	300	—	—	—	3392	—	23	17
Total,	5435	405	5140	16	8369	5000	£ 118 5 0	39	12	57	5	51	—	29	5028	1	60000	175	64595	2	51	30
QUEEN'S COUNTY.																						
First District,	214	62	600	1	—	—	£ 0 5 0	22	7	24	1	17	—	18	2345	3	10000	57	62353	1	38	11
Second District,	250	80	—	1	—	—	—	12	3	16	—	8	1	20	10770	4	110045	60	3692	—	26	5
Third District,	242	38	—	1	—	—	—	12	5	9	1	6	—	9	4714	1	1280000	—	35616	—	30	46
Fourth District,	244	83	—	21	—	—	—	16	5	21	3	11	—	14	3420	2	2500	66	34407	—	34	9
Ch'town & Royalty,	766	247	5500	6	150	1400	100 0 0	3	—	1	—	1	8	10	23000	—	—	358	—	—	300	309
Total,	1716	510	6101	29	150	1400	£ 100 5 0	65	20	70	5	43	9	66	44249	16	1402545	541	141068	1	434	380
Total, P. E. Island	11662	1646	42278	65	12522	6711	£ 368 10 0	145	47	181	13	130	12	116	56787	20	1556245	1207	339498	4	644	479
Total, as per census 1861,	17609	2318	—	—	—	—	—	141	46	176	9	—	—	48	22821	9	1331000	1151	—	—	—	—
Increase,	—	—	—	—	—	—	—	4	1	5	4	—	—	68	33966	11	225245	56	—	—	—	—
Decrease,	5947	672	—	—	—	—	—	—	—	—	—	—	—	—	—	—	—	—	—	—	—	—

NOTE.—In the columns where "increase" and "decrease" both appear blank, no returns were made under these heads in the Census of former years.

4

First Electoral District of Prince County.

NUMBER OF TOWNSHIPS	No. of families	Under 5 years	From 5 to 16	From 16 to 21	From 21 to 45	From 45 to 60	Upwards of 60	Under 5 years	From 5 to 16	From 16 to 21	From 21 to 45	From 45 to 60	Upwards of 60	Deaf and dumb	Blind	No. not vaccinated nor had Small Pox	Total number in each family, including servants and apprentices	No. of married persons in each family	No. of single persons in each family	No. of insane in each family	Married last year	Deaths during the past year	Births during the past year	Males in each family	Females in each family	Members of the Church of England	Presbyterian Church of Lower Provinces	INDIANS	
		MALES.						FEMALES.																					
No. 1,	386	232	364	152	355	127	59	254	343	169	364	90	52	3		2561	2561	786	1775	9	3	11	19			40	75		
No. 2,	211	149	206	64	197	46	29	121	188	82	191	43	25	1	1	974	1343	449	894	5	8	21	40	3	10	91	84		
No. 3,	182	110	172	50	156	57	38	105	179	70	138	44	21			451	1149	322	827	4	5	0	24			139	214		
No. 4,	240	154	205	90	266	50	36	128	172	76	194	59	39	2		526	1460	400	1060	1	1	27	53			181	615		
No. 5,	133	84	131	64	110	52	22	89	121	66	117	38	15	3		462	909	244	665	2	1	8	17	4	5	103	192		
No. 6,	129	98	91	47	105	34	21	80	102	47	107	21	21			460	769	258	511	1		3	39			114	110		
Total,	1281	821	1169	476	1189	366	205	777	1105	510	1114	295	164	9	1	5440	8191	2459	5732	22	18	71	192	7	15	668	1290		

First Electoral District of Prince County, (continued.)

NUMBER OF TOWNSHIPS	Kirk of Scotland	Roman Catholics	Methodists	Baptists	Bible Christians	Quakers Universalists	Other Denominations	No. of acres held in fee simple	No. of acres held by lease, or agreement for lease	No. of acres held by verbal agreement	No. of acres held, as occupants, being neither leaseholders nor leaseholders	No. of persons holding land of First quality	Second quality	Third quality	No. of acres of arable land	No. of bushels of Wheat	No. of bushels of Winter Wheat	No. of bushels of Barley	No. of bushels of Oats	No. of bushels of Buckwheat	No. of bushels of Indian Corn	No. of bushels of Clover Seed	No. of bushels of Timothy Seed	No. of bushels Potatoes
No. 1,	28	2370	22	18			2	21339				191	71	28	19162	10396		1492	55642	608	177	6	18	118720
No. 2,	7	1110	26		24	1		130	10610	367		27	150	12	5088	5224		579	23738	114	134	44	54	46419
No. 3,	6	614	167	1	7		1	14867	2613			64	97	10	6021	5089		1078	89790	1568		12	138	47378
No. 4,		539	111	7	6		1	15776	165	156		62	119	32	4447	5714		1507	25038	1045		114	88	47750
No. 5,	45	456	69	25	6	2	1	11147	200	160		60	47	11	7667	5018	159	1329	15382	989	10	5	72	33580
No. 6,	4	397	38	8	84		8	9344				41	61	21	9316	2387		1067	14473	1484	28½	70½	684	25394
Total,	90	5502	483	59	127	2	4	10	72603	13588	683	208	445	545	114	51701	33178	159	7052	172068	6303	349½	164	428½	319041

First Electoral District of Prince County, (continued.)

NUMBER OF TOWNSHIPS	No. of bushels of Turnips	No. of bushels of other Roots	Apples and other Fruit, (value) £ s. d.	No. of tons of Hay	Number of bushels of Beans	Number of bushels of Peas	Number of bushels of Vetches	Number of pounds of Flax	Number of Flax Manufactories	Number of acres covered with Shell Manure	Number of acres covered with Lime	Pounds of Cheese manufactured during the past year	Pounds of Butter	Number of Fanning Mills	Number of Mowing Machines	Number of Stumping Machines	Number of Hay-making Machines	Number of Hay Elevators	Number of Mud Diggers	Number of other useful Machines	Number of Carts, Trucks and Truck-wagons	Number of Riding Wagons and Carriages, Wood Sleds and Jaunting Sleighs	Number of yards of Cloth manufactured during the past year (fulled)	Number of yards of Cloth manufactured during the past year (not fulled)	Number of Threshing Machines	Number of Horses
No. 1,	2177		14 0 0	670		531		20		150		2182	518	6	1		1				404	690		1972	617	663
No. 2,	2102	3	5 0 0	330	9¼	214½		569		604		630	7687	13	2	1	3		11	6	195	330	2735	6022	9	324
No. 3,	1843		7 7 0	649		16		525			10	12856	8	4		7	2	10	5	169	346	2356	6748	12	336
No. 4,	6610			604	½	7		32	1	604		300	10275	21	10	3	10		33	18	177	412	2122	5495	7	316
No. 5,	2477		3 17 0	327	1	1		163		757		130	1536	5	5	1	2	1	31	1	112	115	1484	4050	13	376
No. 6,	2094	3	36 0 0	162	8	13	1	177		358			4785	5	1				15	2	98	48	3177	3132	10	154
Total,	17303	6	52 18 0	2742	19¼	584½	1	1472	1	2324¼		1220	58904	70	28	5	22		3101	32	1155	1936	11875	45173	68	2169

First Electoral District of Prince County, (continued.)

NUMBER OF TOWNSHIPS	Number of Neat Cattle	Number of Sheep	Number of Hogs	NATIVES OF					Other Countries	Number of Churches	Number of Schoolhouses	Number of Brewing and Distilling Establishments	Number of Tanneries	Pounds of Leather manufactured during the past year	Pounds of Tobacco manufactured during the past year	Number of Fishing Establishments	No. of barrels of Mackerel cured during the past year	No. of barrels of Herring or Alewives	Quintals of Codfish or Hake	No. of Boats owned for fishing purposes	Gallons of Fish Oil made during the past year	No. of men engaged in Fishing	No. of Fish Barrels manufactured during the past year	No. of Coopers' Shops	Pounds of Hake Sounds cured during the past year	Quantity of Preserved Shell and other Fish prepared during the past year	Salmon,—value
				England	Scotland	Ireland	British Provinces	P. E. Island																			
No. 1,	1047	3823	1596	19	14	78	171	2278	1	2	8			12500			50	2885	2136	2295	186	1896	231	1000	1	2390	£150
No. 2,	720	1670	737	5	9	40	18	1270	1		1						8	1084	635	722	57	457	149	1000		250	
No. 3,	831	3619	731	16	14	38	46	1030	5	1	5						2	506	367	234	38	98	51	4050	2		
No. 4,	695	1555	824	30	17	35	85	1286	7	3	4			51900	7		15	2294	1952	2281	75	1201	206	21600	9	1063	
No. 5,	506	1117	444	21	9	10	58	811		2	3						1	140	535	281	26	194	19	2112	2	300	
No. 6,	428	833	446	19	13	14	15	708		1								50	20	3	12	4					
Total,	4827	12617	4478	110	76	215	393	7383	14	8	22			64400	7		76	6909	5575	5813	385	3858	660	29762	14	4003	£150

First Electoral District of Prince County, (concluded.)

NUMBER of TOWNSHIPS	No. of Grist Mills	Mills, whether driven by steam, water or horse power.				No. of Steam Engines, for mechanical or other purposes	No. of Lime Kilns	Barrels of Lime manufactured during the past year	No. of Brick Kilns	No. of Bricks manufactured during the past year	No. of Carriages and Sleighs manufactured during the past year	Yards of Cloth manufactured during the past year	No. of Cloth Factories	No. of Sewing Machines	No. of Pianos, Melodeons and Organs	GENERAL REMARKS
		No. of Carding Mills	No. of Saw Mills	No. of Fulling and Dressing Mills	No. of Shingle and Lath Mills											
No. 1,	2	2	4	2	2											
No. 2,	1	1	2		1				1	90000	42					
No. 3,	4		3		3						15	9104		1		
No. 4,	2		3		1						99	7618		12	12	
No. 5,	1		3		1							25614				
No. 6,	2		1		1							3243				
Total,	12	3	16	2	9				1	90000	156	45579		13	12	

Second Electoral District of Prince County.

NUMBER OF TOWNSHIPS.	No. of families	MALES.						FEMALES.						Deaf and dumb	Blind	No. not vaccinated nor had Small Pox	Total number, including servants and apprentices	No. of married persons	No. of single persons	No. of insane	Married during the past year	Deaths during the past year	Births during the past year		INDIANS.		Members of the Church of Eng. land	Presbyterian Church of Lower Provinces
		Under 5 years	From 5 to 16	From 16 to 21	From 21 to 45	From 45 to 60	Upwards of 60	Under 5 years	From 5 to 16	From 16 to 21	From 21 to 45	From 45 to 60	Upwards of 60											Males	Females		
No. 7,	129	91	127	36	100	28	25	96	134	45	120	29	20	1		705	867	244	623	1	2	6	23			91	101
No. 8,	103	60	102	33	96	27	18	68	87	48	103	26	9			560	672	165	507	1	4	7	20			15	261
No. 9,	67	36	71	36	48	22	9	26	72	36	55	16	4			395	431	112	319	1	1	1	8			14	163
No. 10,	42	17	31	35	89	14	7	30	59	28	47	13	6				376	63	313	1			7			19	79
No. 11,	88	59	86	30	74	25	18	43	87	36	69	22	15			294	570	177	393			6	19			91	122
No. 12,	88	57	89	25	97	25	14	50	50	37	86	21	9			369	560	157	403	1	4	9	29			149	149
No. 13,	200	103	172	59	176	38	32	107	151	62	158	23	22			883	1103	308	795	1	5	10	40	73	78	210	425
Total,	717	423	688	260	686	179	123	420	640	287	638	150	85	1		3206	4570	1226	3353	6	17	39	146	73	78	580	1300

Second Electoral District of Prince County, (continued.)

NUMBER OF TOWNSHIPS	Kirk of Scotland	Roman Catholics	Methodists	Baptists	Bible Christians	Quakers Universalists Other Denominations	No. of acres held in fee simple	No. of acres held by lease, or agreement for lease	No. of acres held by verbal agreement	No. of acres held, as occupants, being neither freeholders nor leaseholders	No. of persons holding land of First quality	Second quality	Third quality	No. of acres of arable land	No. of bushels of Wheat	No. of bushels of Winter Wheat	No. of bushels of Barley	No. of bushels of Oats	No. of bushels of Buckwheat	No. of bushels of Indian Corn	No. of bushels of Clover Seed	No. of bushels of Timothy Seed	No. of bushels Potatoes
No. 7,	1	241	109	64	260		4813	6274½	250		101	17	2	4732	6298	1	944	24463	1830	6	31	112	32818
No. 8,		197	117	1	79	1	13029½	198	135	605	27	53	10	3012	3039	1	588	12922	979	1	26	150	19329
No. 9,	43	196	15				65	2434	2235	140	23	41		1140	806	41	311	4638	285	6	1		9693
No. 10,	1	104	63		47	63	523	3126½	40		1	25	13	1598	715		229	3646	228	2	8½	6½	8705
No. 11,	6	329	4	3	15		10520	2.6			49	24	7	4109	2781		511	12648	419	6	5	98	18661
No. 12,	20	94	16	7	123		2 2056½	6000	789	1	20	36	14	2171	1036		430	8258	711	11	54	23	11092
No. 13,		202	50	20	194		2 5280	8113	1085		93	45	3	6000	4033	15	1209	31435	1397	20	37	58	39188
Total,	71	1363	374	95	718	1	68 36236	26412	4534	946	314	241	49	22762	18708	58	4222	101005	5849	50	114	447½	139486

Second Electoral District of Prince County, (continued.)

NUMBER OF TOWNSHIPS	No. of bushels of Turnips	No. of bushels of other Roots	Apples and other Fruit, (value)	No. of tons of Hay	Number of bushels of Beans	Number of bushels of Peas	Number of bushels of Vetches	Number of pounds of Flax	Number of Flax Manufactories	Number of acres covered with Shell Manure	Number of acres covered with Lime	Pounds of Cheese manufactured during the past year	Pounds of Butter	Number of Fanning Mills	Number of Mowing Machines	Number of Stumping Machines	Number of Hay-making Machines	Number of Hay Elevators	Number of Mud Diggers	Number of other useful Machines	Number of Carts, Trucks and Truck-wagons	Number of Riding Wagons and Carriages, Wood Sleds and Jaunting Sleighs	Number of yards of Cloth manufactured during the past year (fulled)	Number of yards of Cloth manufactured during the past year (not fulled)	Number of Threshing Machines	Number of Horses
No. 7,	2872	36	£17 4	780	14	9½	27					591	10256	13½	4						123	231	1839	5617 17		235
No. 8,	1497	14	34 10	470	16	6½	146	15			260	8066	10	5		4				5 188	78	193	1194	3827 12		175
No. 9,	72			169			87	13				3373	1		1	4				34	17	910	1490 1		80
No. 10,	340	7		132	2	11	76	77				2660	5	1	1					36	67	367	1328 5		66
No. 11,	1182	14½	33 0	404	2	4	400	167	161	837		6539	2	1				16		103	122	1163	3560 3		237
No. 12,	471	6	23 16	321	12	5	180	1	88		251	6907	4	1					6	99	37	155	517	3120 24		129
No. 13,	3315	169	25 4	934	28	50½	193	637		106 1432	14918	14	5					1 25	16	173	313	1564	5239 12		530
Total,	9749 246½		£133 14	3210	74	86½	1,109	1	997	267 3371	52779	49½ 17		6	1	62	303	579	1158	7604	24181 74	1452				

Second Electoral District of Prince County, (continued.)

NUMBER OF TOWNSHIPS.	No. of neat Cattle	No. of Sheep	No. of Hogs	NATIVES OF						No. of Schoolhouses	No. of Brewing and Distilling Establishments	No. of Tanneries	Pounds of Leather manufactured during the past year	Pounds of Tobacco manufactured during the past year	No. of Fishing Establishments	No. of Barrels of Mackerel cured during the past year	No. of Barrels of Herring or Alewives	No. of Quintals of Codfish or Hake	No. of Boats owned for fishing purposes	Gallons of Oil made during the past year	No. of men engaged in Fishing	No. of Fish Barrels manufactured during the past year	No. of Cooper's Shops	Pounds of Hake Sounds cured during the past year	Quantity of Preserved Shell and other fish prepared during the past year
				England	Scotland	Ireland	British Provinces	P. E. Island	Other Countries	No. of Churches																
No. 7,	705	1480	508	22	7	21	30	785	2	4	3					4	1264	100	8	63				
No. 8,	576	1040	592	12	28	6	13	609	4		2		1	1500		2	200	4	7	3	11	90		
No. 9,	187	371	176	3	8	3	4	413	7	6					1	5	341		13			260	1	
No. 10,	212	337	116	9	5	2	13	347	1	2							170	2	8	2				
No. 11,	582	943	236	9	4	52	2	503	3	3				22		10	246	199	5	80	7	152	1	
No. 12,	316	588	200	17	12	6	41	480	1	2	2				1	4	265	233	10	61	11	900	3	
No. 13,	975	1805	595	70	13	10	26	983	1	2	5						686	130	15	50	18			
Total,	3553	6564	2513	142	77	100	132	4120	8	19	23		1	1542		4	23	2034	668	69	257	49	1402	5	

First Electoral District of Prince County, (concluded.)

NUMBER OF TOWNSHIPS.	No. of Grist Mills	No. of Carding Mills	No. of Saw Mills	No. of Fulling and Dressing Mills	No. of Shingle and Lath Mills	No. of Steam Engines, for mechanical or other purposes	No. of Lime Kilns	Barrels of Lime manufactured during the past year	No. of Brick Kilns	No. of Bricks manufactured during the past year	No. of Carriages and Sleighs manufactured during the past year	Yards of Cloth manufactured during the past year	No. of Cloth Factories	No. of Sewing Machines	No. of Pianos, Melodeons and Organs	GENERAL REMARKS.
No. 7,	2	2	4		2						2	7430	1			
No. 8,	2		3		1											
No. 9,			1									2178				
No. 10,			2		2						6	1679	1			
No. 11,	1		1		1							4767				
No. 12,	1	2	2		1						14	2986	4	1		
No. 13,	2		2					1	300			6854	2	1		
Total,	8	4	15		7			1	300		22	25794	8	2		

Third Electoral District of Prince County.

NUMBER or TOWNSHIPS.	MALES.							FEMALES.							Deaf and dumb	Blind	No. not vaccinated nor had Small Pox	Total number, including servants and apprentices	No. of married persons	No. of single persons	No. of insane	Married during the past year	Deaths during the past year	Births during the past year	INDIANS.		Members of the Church of England	Presbyterian Church of the Lower Provinces
	No. of families	Under 5 years	From 5 to 16	From 16 to 21	From 21 to 45	From 45 to 60	Upwards of 60	Under 5 years	From 5 to 16	From 16 to 21	From 21 to 45	From 45 to 60	Upwards of 60											Males	Females		
No. 14,	188	113	217	69	138	65	35	104	192	65	178	56	20	1		1128	1252	355	897	1	8	13	49	5	3	52	189
No. 15,	244	154	204	78	214	84	49	146	205	96	212	77	31	4	1	1547	1550	520	1030	10	1	34	86	10	7	24	74
No. 16,	151	78	146	58	128	43	29	77	129	58	128	39	30			919	931	289	617	1	14	1	30			11	248
No. 18,	175	114	140	63	165	60	35	96	154	66	170	49	29	4		7	1150	307	843	1	3		12	7	3	143	533
Princetown and Royalty.	64	29	49	25	49	23	23	20	57	29	68	30	15			17	417	105	312		1	1	5			16	370
Total,	822	488	765	293	694	275	171	443	737	314	756	242	125	9	2	4012	5300	1571	3720	12	28	58	182	22	13	286	1364

Third Electoral District of Prince County, (continued.)

NUMBER OF TOWNSHIPS	Kirk of Scotland	Roman Catholics	Methodists	Baptists	Bible Christians	Quakers	Universalists	Other Denominations	No. of acres held in fee simple	No. of acres held by lease, or agreement for lease	No. of acres held by verbal agreement	No. of acres held, as occupants, being neither freeholders nor leaseholders	No. of persons holding land of First quality	Second quality	Third quality	No. of acres of arable land	No. of bushels of Wheat	No. of bushels of Winter Wheat	No. of bushels of Barley	No. of bushels of Oats	No. of bushels of Buck wheat	No. of bushels of Indian Corn	No. of bushels of Clover Seed	No. of bushels of Timothy Seed	No. of bushels Potatoes
No. 14,		1046	16	11					8	13526				25	71	89	14	4735	1922		2016	31301	1782	34	20	56	41354
No. 15,		1357	75	17	3					16260	405			891	20	98	99	5245	5015		2531	30615	1877	1495	45	60	51480
No. 16,	75	450	50	39					1	4384	9057	516			15	66	66	4749	2254	172	2914	33720	1703	24	35	131	34085
No. 18,	20	381	22	32	11				8	9652	4613	162			64	84	9	7926	5423		6104	45347	603	2	29	243	43790
Princetown and Royalty		21	7						1	2	4680	282	1		26	26	3	2553	2301		3005	18272	145		7	110	16676
Total,	95	3255	170	88	25				1	19	48522	14557	619		916	196	363	191	25208	16915	172	16650	159255	6110	1555	137	611	187585

7

Third Electoral District of Prince County, (continued.)

NUMBER OF TOWNSHIPS	No. of bushels of Turnips	No. of bushels of other Roots	Apples and other Fruit, (value)	No. of tons of Hay	Number of bushels of Beans	Number of bushels of Peas	Number of bushels of Vetches	Number of pounds of Flax	Number of Flax Manufactories	Number of acres covered with Shell Manure	Number of acres covered with Lime	Pounds of Cheese manufactured during the past year	Pounds of Butter	Number of Fanning Mills	Number of Mowing Machines	Number of Stumping Machines	Number of Haymaking Machines	Number of Hay Elevators	Number of Mud Diggers	Number of Horse-power Machines	Number of Carts, Trucks and Truck-wagons	Number of Riding Wagons and Carriages, Wood Sleds and Jaunting Sleighs	Number of yards of Cloth manufactured during the past year (fulled)	Number of yards of Cloth manufactured during the past year (not fulled)	Number of Threshing Machines	Number of Horses
No. 14,	1721	21	£48 5	672	18¼	24¼		742		27½		6¼	10550	29	2	1		3	2"	4	165	387	2555	5054	13	340
No. 15,	2267		8 17	765	8	48		1710		13		20	6078	13	6	2			7	7	231	396	3918	2220	16	403
No. 16,	2645		6 13	1111		27		270		449		525	10360	32	12	2	11	4	33	2	185	359	2115	3606	20	303
No. 18,	6970		3	1488		2¼		76	1561	123	3. 10	18066	26	21	8	1	9	47	19	185	421	2710	6800	8	408
Princetown and Royalty.	6390		7 15	586	1	11½		43		672	50	3275	8177	9	12	2		4	21	24	90	166	1149	2691	7	162
Total,	19993	21	£64 10	4622	27½	113¼		2847		8067	173	8194	53231	109	53	15	15	17	131	56	857	1730	12447	21271	75	1616

Third Electoral District of Prince County, (continued.)

NUMBER OF TOWNSHIPS.	Number of Neat Cattle	Number of Sheep	Number of Hogs	NATIVES OF England	NATIVES OF Scotland	NATIVES OF Ireland	NATIVES OF British Provinces	P. E. Island	Other Countries	Number of Churches	Number of Schoolhouses	Number of Brewing and Distilling Establishments	Number of Tanneries	Pounds of Leather manufactured during the past year	Pounds of Tobacco manufactured during the past year	Number of Fishing Establishments	No. of barrels of Mackerel cured during the past year	No. of barrels of Herring or Alewives	Quintals of Codfish or Hake	No. of Boats owned for fishing purposes	Gallons of Fish Oil made during the past year	No. of men engaged in Fishing	No. of Fish Barrels manufactured during the past year	No. of Coopers' Shops	Pounds of Hake Sounds cured during the past year	Value of Preserved Shell and other Fish prepared during the past year	Salmon,—value
No. 14,	890	1789	757	10	15	14	28	1185	2	5					208			11½	558	19	8	17						
No. 15,	858	2135	865	7	4	2	51	1480	2	5			1	1000			4	186	1405	120	3½	110	10				
No. 16,	883	1700	556	13	26	15	13	864	3	1	4						8	152	22	4	16						
No. 18,	1040	2642	767	10	19	26	18	1078	2	1	5				70			3	296	244	6	152	9				£21
Princetown and Royalty.	443	1027	389	2	8	10	10	390	2	1	1				100		1	6½	319	212	13	93	9				290
Total,	4064	6393	3284	42	67	64	120	5008	7	7	20		1	1373			5	216	2666	643	67	388	28				£811

Third Electoral District of Prince County, (concluded.)

NUMBER OF TOWNSHIPS	No. of Grist Mills	Mills, whether driven by steam, water or horse power.				No. of Steam Engines, for mechanical or other purposes	No. of Lime Kilns	Barrels of Lime manufactured during the past year	No. of Brick Kilns	No. of Bricks manufactured during the past year	No. of Carriages and Sleighs manufactured during the past year	Yards of Cloth manufactured during the past year	No. of Cloth Factories	No. of Sewing Machines	No. of Pianos, Melodeons and Organs	GENERAL REMARKS.
		No. of Carding Mills	No. of Saw Mills	No. of Fulling and Dressing Mills	No. of Shingle and Lath Mills											
No. 14,	1		2		*1							8509		4		
No. 15,			1				1					5233	1			
No. 16,	1	1	2		1	1	1	10	2	3700	2	5817		2	1	
No. 18,	4	1	3		3			2		500	7	9351		4	1	
Princetown and Royalty.								1		300	2	3774		3		
Total,	6	2	8		5	2	4	810	2	3700	11	33184	1	13	2	

Fourth Electoral District of Prince County.

NUMBER OF TOWNSHIPS.	No. of families	MALES.						FEMALES.						Deaf and dumb	Blind	No. not vaccinated nor had Small Pox	Total number, including servants and apprentices	No. of married persons	No. of single persons	No. of insane	Married during the past year	Deaths during the past year	Births during the past year	INDIANS.		Members of the Church of England	Presbyterian Church of the Lower Provinces
		Under 5 years	From 5 to 16	From 16 to 21	From 21 to 45	From 45 to 60	Upwards of 60	Under 5 years	From 5 to 16	From 16 to 21	From 21 to 45	From 45 to 60	Upwards of 60											Males	Females		
No. 19,	216	112	189	81	190	57	52	115	180	97	198	55	39			674	1371	391	980	4	12	15	41			165	35
No. 25,	150	79	138	39	139	40	26	80	127	62	137	33	25	2	1	437	925	292	633	2	9	16	31	11	18	37	309
No. 26,	194	121	145	61	197	52	50	135	180	68	213	45	28	1		475	1295	378	917	1	8	12	54			19	207
No. 27,	231	113	181	58	148	66	48	116	202	65	159	65	48			402	1260	430	839		4	15	35				70
No. 28,	257	134	235	90	200	82	56	128	216	86	228	73	42			285	1570	583	987		4	10	15			11	179
Total,	1048	559	888	329	880	297	232	574	905	378	935	271	182	3	1	2273	6430	2074	4356	7	37	68	176	11	18	232	1121

Fourth Electoral District of Prince County, (continued.)

NUMBER OF TOWNSHIPS	Kirk of Scotland	Roman Catholics	Methodists	Baptists	Bible Christians	Quakers	Universalists	Other Denominations	No. of acres held in fee simple	No. of acres held by lease, or agreement for lease	No. of acres held by verbal agreement	No. of acres held, as occupants being neither freeholders nor leaseholders	No. of persons holding land of First quality	Second quality	Third quality	No. of acres of arable land	No. of bushels of Wheat	No. of bushels of Winter Wheat	No. of bushels of Barley	No. of bushels of Oats	No. of bushels of Buckwheat	No. of bus. of Indian Corn	No. of bushels of Clover Seed	No. of bushels of Timothy Seed	No. of bushels Potatoes
No. 19,	51	503	202	67	11		9	7	4740	13050	320		8	127	25	9908	4470		3419	61040		14	36	275	63380
No. 25,	46	116	151	176	1			29	15883	554	83	405	42	78	1	10764	4327		1029	78580	3840	0	22	171	49927
No. 26,	72	193	331	162				11	4898	5944		847	136	29	1	872	5149		4605	71320	3667		50	2054	60342
No. 27,	132	674	350	42		1			16614	1149			16	130	43	8727	2073		2001	77381	4175		37	74	55555
No. 29,	379	161	527	210				1,102	9931	6937			121	60		9390	3981		2869	77011	5844	4	1594	4894	63180
Total,	680	2007	1561	657	12	1	10	1,119	52066	27634	403	1252	323	430	70	39607	20003		13923	366332	17520	114	3044	1215	292384

Fourth Electoral District of Prince County, (continued.)

NUMBER OF TOWNSHIPS	No. of bushels of Turnips	No. of bushels of other Roots	Apples and other Fruit, (value)	No. of tons of Hay	Number of bushels of Beans	Number of bushels of Pease	Number of bushels of Vetches	Number of pounds of Flax	Number of Flax Manufactories	Number of acres covered with Shell Manure	Number of acres covered with Lime	Pounds of Cheese manufactured during the past year	Pounds of Butter	Number of Fanning Mills	Number of Mowing Machines	Number of Stumping Machines	Number of Hay-making Machines	Number of Hay Elevators	Number of Mud Diggers	Number of other useful Machines	Number of Carts, Trucks and Truck-wagons	Number of Riding Wagons and Carriages, Wood Sleds and Jaunting Sleighs	Number of yards of Cloth manufactured during the past year (not fulled)	Number of yards of Cloth manufactured during the past year (fulled)	Number of Threshing Machines	Number of Horses
No. 19,	7170	10	£ 29 4	1801	8	11		137		1353	478	2135	22425	80	27	1		9	2	60	2	317	600	3095	6085	47	545
No. 25,	3965	45	128 0	1336	8	10		116		1695	207	3166	25148	78	56	5	1	1	44	51	235	458	2266	5729	48	411
No. 26,	8876	16	321 0	1899	7½	15	4	205		1526	238	1915	30951	73	34	5	9	17	38	47	321	626	1670	6376	40	534
No. 27,	1910	19	12 5	933	2			174		431	124	576	22544	40	8			6	5		233	388	2248	6106	41	464
No. 28,	7370			1511	3			5		2681	2294	1510	25340	66	35	2			2	10	1	347	538	4077	7649	84	518
Total,	29291	90	£ 490 9	7480	29	36	4	637		4886	1165	9302	126403	337	160	13	19	28	157	101	1453	2608	13356	33145	266	2472

Fourth Electoral District of Prince County, (continued.)

NUMBER OF TOWNSHIPS	No. of neat Cattle	No. of Sheep	No. of Hogs	NATIVES OF England	NATIVES OF Scotland	NATIVES OF Ireland	NATIVES OF British Provinces	NATIVES OF P. E. Island	NATIVES OF Other Countries	No. of Churches	No. of Schoolhouses	No. of Brewing and Distilling Establishments	No. of Tanneries	Pounds of Leather manufactured during the past year	Pounds of Tobacco manufactured during the past year	No. of Fishing Establishments	No. of Barrels of Mackerel cured during the past year	No. of Barrels of Herring or Alewives	No. of Quintals of Codfish or Hake	No. of Boats owned for fishing purposes	Gallons of Oil made during the past year	No. of men engaged in Fishing	No. of Fish Barrels manufactured during the past year	No. of Cooper's Shops	Pounds of Hake Sounds cured during the past year	Quantity of Preserved Shell and other fish prepared during the past year
No. 19,	1302	2891	810	62	50	11	28	1185	5	3	5		1	1	125					105	15	8	8	4		
No. 25,	1139	2559	714	22	32	30	17	824	2	2	4				81											
No. 26,	1231	3302	994	23	13	102	63	1089	5	2	5			3	6708	1	3				4					
No. 27,	1116	2521	608	30	10	164	28	1631	3	4	4													1		
No. 28,	1463	3887	610	29	37	25	25	1453	1	5	6										2					
Total,	6251	15160	3826	166	142	362	161	5585	14	16	24	1	4	6914			1	3	105	15	14	8	4	1		

Fourth Electoral District of Prince County, (concluded.)

NUMBER OF TOWNSHIPS	No. of Grist Mills	No. of Carding Mills	No. of Saw Mills	No. of Fulling and Dressing Mills	No. of Shingle and Lath Mills	No. of Steam Engines, for mechanical or other purposes	No. of Lime Kilns	Barrels of Lime manufactured during the past year	No. of Brick Kilns	No. of Bricks manufactured during the past year	No. of Carriages and Sleighs manufactured during the past year	Yards of Cloth manufactured during the past year	No. of Cloth Factories	No. of Sewing Machines	No. of Pianos, Melodeons and Organs	GENERAL REMARKS
No. 19,	2	3	1	1							113	9889	3	1		
No. 25,	3		5		3				2	100	19	7995	10	1		
No. 26,	6	2	5		2				8	2400	22		29	13		
No. 27,			1								12		9	4		
No. 28,	2		2		2				3	1700	38	11354	8			
Total,	13	5	14	1	14				13	4200	195	29278	59	19		

Fifth Electoral District of Prince County.

NUMBER OF TOWNSHIPS	No. of families	MALES.						FEMALES.						Deaf and dumb	Blind	No. not vaccinated nor had Small Pox	Total number, including servants and apprentices	No. of married persons	No. of single persons	No. of insane	Married during the past year	Deaths during the past year	Births during the past year	INDIANS.		Members of the Church of England	Presbyterian Church of the Lower Provinces
		Under 5 years	From 6 to 16	From 16 to 21	From 21 to 45	From 45 to 60	Upwards of 60	Under 5 years	From 6 to 16	From 16 to 21	From 21 to 45	From 45 to 60	Upwards of 60											Males	Females		
No. 17,	235	153	227	88	220	80	43	118	270	123	218	70	34		3	854	1644	452	1192	2	7	7	46			160	195
Summerside,	307	186	237	95	305	110	28	180	251	130	321	47	27	1		536	1917	580	1337	2	4	24	74	1		307	463
Total,	542	339	464	183	525	190	71	298	521	253	539	117	61	1	3	1890	3561	1032	2529	4	11	31	120	1		767	658

Fifth Electoral District of Prince County, (continued.)

NUMBER OF TOWNSHIPS	Kirk of Scotland	Roman Catholics	Methodists	Baptists	Bible Christians	Quakers	Universalists	Other Denominations	No. of acres held in fee simple	No. of acres held by lease, or agreement for lease	No. of acres held by verbal agreement	No. of acres held, as occupants, being neither freeholders nor leaseholders	No. of persons holding land of First quality	Second quality	Third quality	No. of acres of arable land	No. of bushels of Wheat	No. of bushels of Winter Wheat	No. of bushels of Barley	No. of bushels of Oats	No. of bushels of Buck wheat	No. of bus. of Indian Corn	No. of bushels of Clover Seed	No. of bushels of Timothy Seed	No. of bushels Potatoes
No. 17,	28	735	120	26		2	2	74	14943	2671	80		86	43	5	6587	4422		3915	53327	3341	95	834	1764	66801
Summerside,	95	605	229	115	14		23	66	1418	50			12			946	710	150	257	3295	130		2	10	3620
Total,	123	1340	349	143	14	2	25	140	16361	2721	80		98	43	5	7533	5132	150	4172	56622	3471	95	854	1864	70421

Fifth Electoral District of Prince County, (continued.)

NUMBER OF TOWNSHIPS.	No. of bushels of Turnips	No. of bushels of other Roots	Apples and other Fruit, (value)	No. of tons of Hay	Number of bushels of Beans	Number of bushels of Peas	Number of bushels of Vetches	Number of pounds of Flax	Number of Flax Manufactories	Number of acres covered with Shell Manure	Number of acres covered with Lime	Pounds of Cheese manufactured during the past year	Pounds of Butter	Number of Fanning Mills	Number of Mowing Machines	Number of Stumping Machines	Number of Hay-making Machines	Number of Hay Elevators	Number of Mud Diggers	Number of other useful Machines	Number of Carts, Trucks and Truck-wagons	Number of Riding Wagons and Carriages, Wood Sleds and Jaunting Sleighs	Number of yards of Cloth manufactured during the past year (fulled)	Number of yards of Cloth manufactured during the past year (not fulled)	Number of Threshing Machines	Number of Horses
No. 17,	6808		£7 0 0	1957	10½	314		427		1044	1504	350	21025	42	35	3	8	6	38	378	298	580	2537	10405	34	458
Summerside,	320	20		252						64	34		1250	7	4			4	3	28	86	216	60	309	4	104
Total,	7128	20	£7 0 0	2209	10½	314		427		1108	1844	350	22275	49	39	3	8	10	41	406	384	796	2597	10712	38	562

Fifth Electoral District of Prince County, (continued.)

NUMBER OF TOWNSHIPS.	No. of neat Cattle	No. of Sheep	No. of Hogs	NATIVES OF					No. of Schoolhouses	No. of Churches	No. of Brewing and Distilling Establishments	No. of Tanneries	Pounds of Leather manufactured during the past year	Pounds of Tobacco manufactured during the past year	No. of Fishing Establishments	No. of Barrels of Mackerel cured during the past year	No. of Barrels of Herring or Alewives	No. of Quintals of Codfish or Hake	No. of Boats owned for fishing purposes	Gallons of Oil made during the past year	No. of men engaged in Fishing	No. of Fish Barrels manufactured during the past year	No. of Cooper's Shops	Pounds of Hake Sounds cured during the past year	Quantity of Preserved Shell and other fish prepared during the past year	No. of Salmon taken during the past year, and the value thereof
				England	Scotland	Ireland	British Provinces	P. E. Island	Other Countries																		
No. 17,	960	2590	960	53	20	23	60	1483	5	2	7		2	5000													
Summerside,	192	180	202	41	36	39	181	1595	25	6	3	2	1	5000	7500												
Total,	1152	2770	1162	94	56	62	241	3078	30	8	10	2	3	10000	7500												

Fifth Electoral District of Prince County, (concluded.)

NUMBER OF TOWNSHIPS	Mills, whether driven by steam, water or horse power.					No. of Steam Engines, for mechanical or other purposes	No. of Lime Kilns	Barrels of Lime manufactured during the past year	No. of Brick Kilns	No. of Bricks manufactured during the past year	No. of Carriages and Sleighs manufactured during the past year	Yards of Cloth manufactured during the past year	No. of Cloth Factories	No. of Sewing Machines	No. of Pianos, Melodeons and Organs	GENERAL REMARKS
	No. of Grist Mills	No. of Carding Mills	No. of Saw Mills	No. of Fulling and Dressing Mills	No. of Shingle and Lath Mills											
No. 17,	1	1	1		1					2	2200		57		20	12
Summerside,	1					1	1			1			50		46	22
Total,	2	1	1		1	1	1			3	2200		107		66	34

First Electoral District of Queen's County.

NUMBER OF TOWNSHIPS	No. of families	MALES.						FEMALES.						Deaf and dumb	Blind	No. not vaccinated nor had Small Pox	Total number, including servants and apprentices	No. of married persons	No. of single persons	No. of insane	Married during the past year	Deaths during the past year	Births during the past year	INDIANS.		Members of the Church of England	Presbyterian Church of the Lower Provinces
		Under 5 years	From 5 to 16	From 16 to 21	From 21 to 45	From 45 to 60	Upwards of 60	Under 5 years	From 5 to 16	From 16 to 21	From 21 to 45	From 45 to 60	Upwards of 60											Males	Females		
No. 20,	201	102	196	55	170	57	48	85	152	78	201	61	40	2	3	753	1245	347	898	3	7	22	36			844	509
No. 21,	249	120	228	81	219	72	40	148	209	85	246	70	42	2	1	1048	1569	459	1110		5	20	43			24	905
No. 22,	223	107	185	92	211	67	54	102	180	96	194	67	46	1		1048	1411	391	1020		13	12	30			50	570
No. 29,	307	172	282	126	249	99	53	175	287	121	259	88	46	2	2	701	1951	535	1422	3	3	28	46			219	247
No. 30,	240	122	229	74	164	77	54	109	197	97	188	78	41	1	2	904	1430	410	1020			9	13			39	273
No. 67,	218	125	234	85	205	48	43	132	185	93	203	56	24		1	1117	1435	367	1008	1	7	15	45			92	876
Total,	1438	748	1354	513	1218	420	301	751	1220	570	1291	422	239	8	9	5571	9047	2509	6538	7	35	106	213			990	3446

First Electoral District of Queen's County, (continued.)

NUMBER OF TOWNSHIPS	Kirk of Scotland	Roman Catholics	Methodists	Baptists	Bible Christians	Quakers	Universalists	Other Denominations	No. of acres held in fee simple	No. of acres held by lease, or agreement for lease	No. of acres held by verbal agreement	No. of acres held, as occupants, being neither freeholders nor leaseholders	No. of persons holding land of First quality	Second quality	Third quality	No. of acres of arable land	No. of bushels of Wheat	No. of bushels of Winter Wheat	No. of bushels of Barley	No. of bushels of Oats	No. of bushels of Buck-wheat	No. of bushels of Indian Corn	No. of bushels of Clover Seed	No. of bushels of Timothy Seed	No. of bushels Potatoes
No. 20,		193	131	4				1	8772	6750		12	8	131	41	7857	6936		3812	54386	873	14	31	2804	57009
No. 21,	2	170	176	31	2		1	32	16230	76	3		100	60	32	8340	7770		3931	50363	1073		1137	2714	56984
No. 22,	18	606	86	64	11				2738	15246	102	523	29	193		7558	5412		5812	61950	1100	2	703	133	55980
No. 29,	313	563	408	133	1	1		14	265	16737	126	1681	28	215	9	10711	3841		2650	83858	1455	2	69	219	72263
No. 30,	518	472	29	32	1				5444	9460	200	2904	50	67	98	5777	2115	50	1643	47912	3310	6	5	52	52814
No. 61,	89	239	80	46				13	12224	10692	492	150	30	198	4	9609	3865		1176	70191	2918		114	1184	53885
Total,	1060	2243	913	313	20	1	1	60	45673	58961	923	5270	254	864	184	49882	29939	50	19183	377603	10750	24	1956	1074	348935

First Electoral District of Queen's County, (continued.)

NUMBER OF TOWNSHIPS	No. of bushels of Turnips	No. of bushels of other Roots	Apples and other Fruit (value)	No. of tons of Hay	Number of bushels of Beans	Number of bushels of Peas	Number of bushels of Vetches	Number of pounds of Flax	Number of Flax Manufactories	Number of acres covered with Shell Manure	Number of acres covered with Lime	Pounds of Cheese manufactured during the past year	Pounds of Butter	Number of Fanning Mills	Number of Mowing Machines	Number of Stumping Machines	Number of Hay-making Machines	Number of Hay Elevators	Number of Mud Diggers	Number of other useful Machines	Number of Carts, Trucks and Truck-wagons	Number of Riding Waggons and Carriages, Wood Sleds and Jaunting Sleighs	Number of yards of Cloth manufactured during the past year (fulled)	Number of yards of Cloth manufactured during the past year (not fulled)	Number of Threshing Machines	Number of Horses
No. 20,	8642	25½	£ s. d 79 2 0	1490	14½	10		1094		1267	81	2805	15201	37	18	2			46	6	215	511	3103	9088	26	471
No. 21,	4665		2 4 0	1473	2	3				1977	364	2500	19065	30	25	3	1	13	69		213	497	3254	7698	22	510
No. 22,	8950	12	45 15 0	1280	3	1		228		1146	44½	2875	16510	10	13	2	2	5	39	14	148	457	2812	6911	26	482
No. 29,	5511	102	34 15 0	1152	18½	6½		676		600	320	1580	26742	84	15	4	4	5	28		337	690	8299	8632	57	586
No. 30,	1718	10	10 10 0	747				156		341	41½	1400	14340	23	9	6	29	2	888	209	364	1000	5185	20	378
No. 67,	6097	67	33 0 0	793	6			638		102	182½	613	16073	30	14	1			2	11	226	426	3384	7783	28	483
Total,	34993	216½	205 7 0	7285	44	20½		1892½		5523	1105½	11838	108946	223	9	118	36	25	183	419	1318	2945	16852	45292	179	2860

First Electoral District of Queen's County, (continued.)

NUMBER OF TOWNSHIPS.	Number of Neat Cattle	Number of Sheep	Number of Hogs	Natives of England	Natives of Scotland	Natives of Ireland	Natives of British Provinces	Natives of P. é. Island	Natives of Other Countries	Number of Churches	Number of Schoolhouses	Number of Brewing and Distilling Establishment	Number of Tanneries	Pounds of Leather manufactured during the past year	Pounds of Tobacco manufactured during the past year	No. of Fishing Establishments	No. of barrels of Mackerel cured during the past year	No. of barrels of Herring or Alewives	Quintals of Codfish or Hake	No. of Boats owned for fishing purposes	Gallons of Fish Oil made during the past year	No. of men engaged in Fishing	No. of Fish Barrels manufactured during the past year	No. of Coopers' Shops	Pounds of Hake Sounds cured during the past year	Value of Preserved Shell and other Fish prepared during the past year	No. of Salmon taken during the past year, and the value thereof
No. 20.	970	2745	794	25	67	22	35	1091	5	1	5			125		26	170	74	6	59	2						
No. 21,	902	2845	1027	34	156	37	13	1324	5	5	4					5 310	473	279	18	141	40						
No. 22,	1076	2715	1062	8	137	102	2	1162		2	8		1	1200		3 251	117	27	10	20	20						
No. 29,	1385	3120	1110	71	50	158	62	1600	7	6	7		3	1550		38	259		12			600	1		1 at £0 5		
No. 30,	956	2264	812	12	134	150	8	1120	2	1	6			1,3500		3	304	9	10								
No. 67,	1186	2795	1099	6	211	55	14	1119.	4	7																	
Total,	6574	16484	5904	156	794	524	129	7425	19	19	37		6	6555		6 628	1823	389	56	214	62	600	1		1	£0 5	

First Electoral District of Queen's County, (concluded.)

NUMBER OF TOWNSHIPS	No. of Grist Mills	No. of Carding Mills	No. of Saw Mills	No. of Fulling and Dressing Mills	No. of Shingle and Lath Mills	No. of Steam Engines, for mechanical or other purposes	No. of Lime Kilns	Barrels of Lime manufactured during the past year	No. of Brick Kilns	No. of Bricks manufactured during the past year	No. of Carriages and Sleighs manufactured during the past year	Yards of Cloth manufactured during the past year	No. of Cloth Factories	No. of Sewing Machines	No. of Pianos, Melodeons and Organs	GENERAL REMARKS
No. 20,	4	1	1				1	15			7	12192	2	4	1	
No. 21,	4		5		3		2	1000				11137		5	1	
No. 22,	3	2	4		1		2					9680		5	1	
No. 29,	8	3	6	1	8		8	1330	1	10000	50	11931		14	7	
No. 30,	1	1	2		1							7428		2	1	
No. 07,	2		6		4							9985		8		
Total,	22	7	24	1	17		13	2345	3	10000	57	62353	1	38	11	

Second Electoral District of Queen's County.

NUMBER OF TOWNSHIPS.	No. of families	MALES.						FEMALES.						Deaf and dumb	Blind	No. not vaccinated nor had Small Pox	Total number, including servants and apprentices	No. of married persons	No. of single persons	No. of insane	Married during the past year	Deaths during the past year	Births during the past year	INDIANS.		Members of the Church of England	Presbyterian Church of the Lower Provinces
		Under 5 years	From 5 to 16	From 16 to 21	From 21 to 45	From 45 to 60	Upwards of 60	Under 5 years	From 5 to 16	From 16 to 21	From 21 to 45	From 45 to 60	Upwards of 60											Males	Females		
No. 23,	291	150	255	109	250	85	39	146	281	117	256	80	36	1	1	220	1804	525	1279	3	4	11	32			79	465
No. 24,	352	193	314	165	320	120	75	177	322	135	344	122	69	5	1	1844	2356	690	1666	4	18	24	78			258	348
No. 31,	203	101	171	88	156	85	49	85	149	128	141	95	30	3	1	402	1278	306	912	3	10	18	33			124	266
No. 32,	210	84	180	75	193	61	54	102	162	90	170	69	36	2	3	725	1276	384	892	3	10	11	33			357	115
No. 65,	275	132	243	132	202	111	59	139	240	154	195	88	51	3		710	1746	453	1293	2	6	19	33	15	20	52	386
Total,	1331	660	1163	569	1121	462	276	649	1154	624	1106	454	222	11	6	3901	8460	2418	6042	15	48	83	209	15	20	870	1580

Second Electoral District of Queen's County, (continued.)

NUMBER OF TOWNSHIPS	Kirk of Scotland	Roman Catholics	Methodists	Baptists	Bible Christians	Quakers	Universalists	Other Denominations	No. of acres held in fee simple	No. of acres held by lease, or agreement for lease	No. of acres held by verbal agreement	No. of acres held, as occupants, being neither freeholders nor leaseholders	No. of persons holding land of First quality	Second quality	Third quality	No. of acres of arable land	No. of bushels of Wheat	No. of bushels of Winter Wheat	No. of bushels of Barley	No. of bushels of Oats	No. of bushels of Buckwheat	No. of bus. of Indian Corn	No. of bushels of Clover Seed	No. of bushels of Timothy Seed	No. of bushels Potatoes
No. 23,	117	670	17	213	207				36	8491	9510	103	50	53	152	9	11310	10033	31	6064	80416	728 15	53	290	78465
No. 24,	237	1300	42	111	46				14	3738	11553	1090		91	176	18	12122	10374		0062	100712	1129 35	18	126	98289
No. 31,	194	225	329	135	1				4	10681	5704	684	607	124	62	2	5848	7540	37	2051	73875	2189	11	238½	85860
No. 32,	209	122	262	163	44				4	16205	2296	94		71	94	9	11168	7098	34	6535	86550	1198		279½	82890
No. 65,	691	403	45	154	11				4	5937	12890			244			9087	7900		2597	70040	857		41	103945
Total,	1448	2720	695	776	309				62	47052	41933	1971	657	583	484	38	50135	42945	102	5090	411393	6101 50	101½	977	449449

12

Second Electoral District of Queen's County, (continued.)

NUMBER of TOWNSHIPS.	No. of bushels of Turnips	No. of bushels of other Roots	Apples and other Fruit, (value)	No. of tons of Hay	Number of bushels of Beans	Number of bushels of Peas	Number of bushels of Vetches	Number of pounds of Flax	Number of Flax Manufactories	Number of acres covered with Shell Manure	Number of acres covered with Lime	Pounds of Cheese manufactured during the past year	Pounds of Butter	Number of Fanning Mills	Number of Mowing Machines	Number of Stumping Machines	Number of Hay-making Machines	Number of Hay Elevators	Number of Mud Diggers	Number of other useful Machines	Number of Carts, Trucks and Truck-wagons	Number of Riding Wagons and Carriages, Wool Sleds and Jaunting Sleighs	Number of yards of Cloth manufactured during the past year (fulled)	Number of yards of Cloth manufactured during the past year (not fulled)	Number of Threshing Machines	Number of Horses
			£ s. d																							
No. 28,	12965	89	59 7 9	2046 2¼	50	166		528		622	10135	28123	50	34 6			10	41	4	274	616	3164	7733	59	506
No. 24,	13065			2077 1	18	555		1720		507	2882	19965	65	34 14			4	77		312	755	4793	11610	68	710
No. 31,	8007	107	35 10 0	1889	25	126		1871		797	4422	29600	48	21 4			4	1	45654	278	498	3437	6413	40	460
No. 32,	33880		3 101 0 0	2865	8	22 30		3453	21	42½	11760	35575	64	65 2			4	3	73 18	330	552	2842	5815	51	540
No. 65,	6840			1718				2157		47	1110	25525	6	18 1			39	1	79	331	511	3301	7519	12	578
Total,	74757	199	285 17 0	10597 3¼	101	22 877		10029	41	15¼	30309	138788	233	172 27			51	15	315 676 1525	2082	17537	39000		230	2886

Second Electoral District of Queen's County, (continued.)

NUMBER OF TOWNSHIPS	Number of Neat Cattle	Number of Sheep	Number of Hogs	NATIVES OF					Number of Churches	Number of Schoolhouses	Number of Brewing and Distilling Establishments	Number of Tanneries	Pounds of Leather manufactured during the past year	Pounds of Tobacco manufactured during the past year	No. of Fishing Establishments	No. of barrels of Mackerel cured during the past year	No. of barrels of Herring or Alewives	Quintals of Codfish or Hake	No. of Boats owned for fishing purposes	Gallons of Fish Oil made during the past year	No. of men engaged in Fishing	No. of Fish Barrels manufactured during the past year	No. of Coopers' Shops	Pounds of Hake Sounds cured during the past year	Value of Preserved Shell and other Fish prepared during the past year	No. of Salmon taken during the past year, and the value thereof
				England	Scotland	Ireland	British Provinces	P. E. Island	Other Countries																	
No. 23,	1262	3115	1296	71	103	19	12	1596	3	5	9					1	60¼	12	20	2	10	4				
No. 24,	1515	4138	1655	52	74	26	31	2173	3	7		1	600			8	554	417	118	23	240	70				
No. 31,	1200	2845	831	65	64	68	12	1069	5	5																
No. 32,	1295	3286	999	54	41	24	17	1135	5	5	7												1			
No. 65,	1362	3473	905	27	109	73	8	1526	3	4	10															
Total,	6834	10857	5686	269	391	210	80	7499	11	22	38	1	600			9	614¼	429	138	25	250	80	1			

Second Electoral District of Queen's County, (concluded.)

NUMBER OF TOWNSHIPS	No. of Grist Mills	No. of Carding Mills	No. of Saw Mills	No. of Fulling and Dressing Mills	No. of Shingle and Lath Mills	No. of Steam Engines, for mechanical or other purposes	No. of Lime Kilns	Barrels of Lime manufactured during the past year	No. of Brick Kilns	No. of Bricks manufactured during the past year	No. of Carriages and Sleighs manufactured during the past year	Yards of Cloth manufactured during the past year	No. of Cloth Factories	No. of Sewing Machines	No. of Pianos, Melodeons and Organs	GENERAL REMARKS
No. 23,	3	1	2		1		1	3		2	30000	53	8692	9	1	
No. 24,	2							3			4600				2	
No. 31,	2		1	10	5										2	
No. 32,	5		1	4	2			P		1	4860	45	7		11	3
No. 65,								6		1	1310	80000			3	1
Total,	12	3	16		8	1	20	10770	4		110045	60	8692	20	5	

Third Electoral District of Queen's County.

NUMBER OF TOWNSHIPS.	No. of families	MALES.						FEMALES.						Deaf and dumb	Blind	No. not vaccinated nor had Small Pox	Total number, including servants and apprentices	No. of married persons	No. of single persons	No. of insane	Married during the past year	Deaths during the past year	Births during the past year	INDIANS.		Members of the Church of England	Presbyterian Church of the Lower Provinces
		Under 5 years	From 5 to 16	From 16 to 21	From 21 to 45	From 45 to 60	Upwards of 60	Under 5 years	From 5 to 16	From 16 to 21	From 21 to 45	From 45 to 60	Upwards of 60											Males	Females		
No. 33,	185	87	189	76	155	63	39	92	176	82	166	57	37			624	1219	373	846	2	7	11	33			144	158
No. 34,	216	122	189	74	207	64	42	98	182	83	218	55	53			596	1387	401	986	1	0	9	28			44	283
No. 35,	179	81	152	66	147	59	40	62	156	90	147	59	21			711	1080	284	796		6	11	36	3	4	16	26
No. 36,	210	110	191	101	219	96	66	97	214	96	198	88	54	1		639	1530	103	1127		10	15	39			17	21
No. 37,	208	115	188	74	161	92	45	104	183	104	177	75	37			610	1355	378	977			2	16			62	219
No. 48,	214	96	204	126	166	98	37	74	191	125	195	70	30	1	1	632	1412	367	1045		13	2	23	9	12	38	47
Total,	1212	611	1113	517	1055	472	269	527	1102	580	1101	404	232	2	1	3815	7983	2206	5777	3	45	50	175	12	16	321	756

13

Third Electoral District of Queen's County, (continued.)

NUMBER OF TOWNSHIPS.	Kirk of Scotland	Roman Catholics	Methodists	Baptists	Bible Christians	Quakers	Universalists	Other Denominations	No. of acres held in fee simple	No. of acres held by lease, or agreement for lease	No. of acres held by verbal agreement	No. of acres held, as occupants, being neither freeholders nor leaseholders	No. of persons holding land of First quality	Second quality	Third quality	No. of acres of arable land	No. of bushels of Wheat	No. of bushels of Winter Wheat	No. of bushels of Barley	No. of bushels of Oats	No. of bushels of Buckwheat	No. of bus. of Indian Corn	No. of bushels of Clover Seed	No. of bushels of Timothy Seed	No. of bushels Potatoes
No. 33,	342	90	160	7	318				7823	9352	50	50	50	90	29	11421	6633		10514	91190	1246	98	362		68000
No. 34,	268	34	318	90	2			10	10761	9453		50	48	126	16	13160	6613	30	5207	91150	304	60	263		85940
No. 35,	80	859	70	27					1543	13145			26	95	41	7333	3884		2362	53565	280	16	111		50392
No. 36,	3	1469	5	1				14	1635	11178	1303		60	80	50	6923	2760		1080	70000	255	10	45	11	29905
No. 37,	16	1040	10	3				8	12195	4776			42	102	27	1959	3220	126	1818	37260	348	10	36		47255
No. 48,	328	388	318	287	6				5721	10857	130		28	92	50	9014	5028	8	2352	65261	383	17	197		73489
Total,	1037	4188	911	415	326			29	39678	59061	1573	100	263	585	207	52810	29147	164	23333	408426	2825	20	202		954354982

Third Electoral District of Queen's County, (continued.)

NUMBER OF TOWNSHIPS	No. of bushels of Turnips	No. of bushels of other Roots	Apples and other Fruit, (value)	No. of tons of Hay	Number of bushels of Beans	Number of bushels of Peas	Number of bushels of Vetches	Number of pounds of Flax	Number of Flax Manufactories	Number of acres covered with Shell Manure	Number of acres covered with Lime	Pounds of Cheese manufactured during the past year	Pounds of Butter	Number of Fanning Mills	Number of Mowing Machines	Number of Stamping Machines	Number of Hay-making Machines	Number of Hay Elevators	Number of Mud Diggers	Number of other useful Machines	Number of Carts, Trucks and Truck-wagons	Number of Riding Wagons and Carriages, Wood Sleds and Jaunting Sleighs	Number of yards of Cloth manufactured during the past year (fulled)	Number of yards of Cloth manufactured during the past year (not fulled)	Number of Threshing Machines	Number of Horses
			£ s. d																							
No. 33,	38024	116	300 0 0	2883	11	52	60			702	3529	5555	28863	84	64	13	88	2	35	42	290	358	3069	4653	88	554
No. 34,	18190		282 0 0	2286	9					876	2754	4510	29400	94	63	2	63	2	47	9	316	645	2818	4980	78	570
No. 35,	3808	4	14 0 0	749	4	5	309			115	110	4450	16733	31	23	1	95		36		315	542	2232	4488	35	350
No. 36,	2720		39 0 0	385			412	1	78	26	670	13283	3	4	1	3		26	1	198	297	3067	4156	10	363
No. 37,	3227	6	62 0 0	290	4	14	217			140	61	2530	9222	5	5	3			14	13	175	385	2346	3087	21	355
No. 48,	10365		102 0 0	1400						415	14	3836	17358	40	33	2			28	1	303	227	2808	4581	23	372
Total,	76334	126	799 0 0	7443	28	71	998	1	2326	6494	21551	114854	257	192	22	190	4	186	66	1633	2454	16340	26195	250	2576

Third Electoral District of Queen's County, (continued.)

NUMBER OF TOWNSHIPS	No. of neat Cattle	No. of Sheep	No. of Hogs	NATIVES OF England	NATIVES OF Scotland	NATIVES OF Ireland	NATIVES OF British Provinces	NATIVES OF P. E. Island	NATIVES OF Other Countries	No. of Churches	No. of Schoolhouses	No. of Brewing and Distilling Establishments	No. of Tanneries	Pounds of Leather manufactured during the past year	Pounds of Tobacco manufactured during the past year	No. of Fishing Establishments	No. of Barrels of Mackerel cured during the past year	No. of Barrels of Herring or Alewives	No. of Quintals of Codfish or Hake	No. of Boats owned for fishing purposes	Galls of fish Oil made during the past year	No. of men engaged in Fishing	No. of Fish Barrels manufactured during the past year	Pounds of Hake Sounds cured during the past year	Quantity of Preserved Shell and other fish prepared during the past year and its value	No. of Salmon taken during the past year, and the value thereof
No. 33,	1304	2249	898	104	46	12	23	1033	1	8	6					2		2	219	12		9	125 12			
No. 34,	1310	3283	1910	42	40	47	14	1210	4	4	4			2	2000	5	365	219	166		5	6 5			
No. 35,	971	2154	705	5	21	105	12	937	1	3								48	270	40	5	6 5			
No. 36,	865	1790	722	2	31	223	16	1257	1	2	4							66	191		10	10			
No. 37,	721	1879	1820	15	6	86	12	1236		1	7			1	2800	2	536	500	230	10	111	11	1		
No. 48,	895	3162	474	26	37	59	21	1268	1	2	4			2	6000										
Total,	6136	15526	6529	194	181	532	98	6971	7	17	28			5	10800	7	717	1180	418	43	242	38	1		

Third Electoral District of Queen's County, (concluded.)

NUMBER OF TOWNSHIPS	Mills, whether driven by steam, water or horse power.						Barrels of Lime manufactured during the past year	No. of Lime Kilns	No. of Bricks manufactured during the past year	No. of Brick Kilns	No. of Carriages and Sleighs manufactured during the past year	Yards of Cloth manufactured during the past year	No. of Cloth Factories	No. of Sewing Machines	No. of Pianos, Melodeons and Organs	GENERAL REMARKS.
	No. of Grist Mills	No. of Carding Mills	No. of Saw Mills	No. of Fulling and Dressing Mills	No. of Shingle and Lath Mills	No. of Steam Engines, for mechanical or other purposes										
No. 33,	2	1	1	1	2		5	3214				7617		14	31	
No. 34,	4	1	1												3	2	
No. 35,													6688				
No. 36,													7223		2	2	
No. 37,	3	1	3		3		2	1000				5691		6	2	
No. 48,	3	2	3		1		2	500	7	1280000		8337		11	0	
Total,	12	5	8	1	6		9	4714	7	1280000		35616		36	40	

Fourth Electoral District of Queen's County.

NUMBER OF TOWNSHIPS	No. of families	MALES.						FEMALES.						Deaf and dumb	Blind	No. not vaccinated nor had Small Pox	Total number, including servants and apprentices	No. of married persons	No. of single persons	No. of insane	Married during the past year	Deaths during the past year	Births during the past year		INDIANS.		Members of the Church of England	Presbyterian Church of the Lower Provinces
		Under 5 years	From 5 to 16	From 16 to 21	From 21 to 45	From 45 to 60	Upwards of 60	Under 5 years	From 5 to 16	From 16 to 21	From 21 to 45	From 45 to 60	Upwards of 60											Males	Females		
No. 49,	240	108	250	06	209	82	52	142	227	138	223	75	59	2		537	1661	436	1225	1	8	8	40			47	
No. 50,	226	114	207	105	182	79	58	86	212	114	217	89	48			699	1511	373	1138	2	8	12	29			208	16
No. 57,	305	163	263	108	232	102	75	134	253	117	300	102	73	1	4	1115	1934	504	1430	6	24	25	51	6	8	18	322
No. 58,	183	105	167	69	159	85	48	84	165	91	186	71	48			849	1258	372	886	3	7	15	32			1	200
No. 60,	167	71	140	39	122	54	35	76	136	54	155	40	39	1		637	901	311	650		1	8	29				417
No. 62,	143	64	135	56	142	45	32	68	121	86	131	49	23	2	1	822	932	237	715	1	23	8	25			4	420
Total.	1264	625	1161	473	1046	427	300	590	1115	600	1221	426	290	5	6	4659	8277	2233	6044	13	77	76	206	6	8	278	1381

Fourth Electoral District of Queen's County, (continued.)

NUMBER OF TOWNSHIPS	Kirk of Scotland	Roman Catholics	Methodists	Baptists	Bible Christians	Quakers	Universalists	Other Denominations	No. of acres held in fee simple	No. of acres held by lease, or agreement for lease	No. of acres held by verbal agreement	No. of acres held, as occupants, being neither freeholders nor leaseholders	No. of persons holding land of First quality	Second quality	Third quality	No. of acres of arable land	No. of bushels of Wheat	No. of bushels of Winter Wheat	No. of bushels of Barley	No. of bushels of Oats	No. of bushels of Buck wheat	No. of bus. of Indian Corn	No. of bushels of Clover Seed	No. of bushels of Timothy Seed	No. of bushels Potatoes
No. 49,	289	831	316	127	29		22		19039	707	202		101	84	39	10079	4911		2915	86767	601	12	17	360	84680
No. 50,	420	541	111	44	159			3	8998	7216	141	287	91	90	25	9526	5283		3175	84862	485	4	66	261	89413
No. 57,	1010	432		9	101	42			21609	316			60	185	30	11493	5216		1684	84197	589	3		289	73357
No. 58,	769	255		24					14743	356	10	198	28	84	71	5273	2885		633	42390	128			120	35050
No. 60,	491	39	4	10					15428		84		52	105	7	4628	1570		339	29742	25			85	24438
No. 62,	403	21		25				79	13864	4	153		20	57	62	5234	2008		991	26067	379	2	5	62	24460
Total,	3391	2119	440	351	230		22	82	93681	8509	540	485	352	605	234	46831	21903		9737	354925	2207	21	88	1186	332298

Fourth Electoral District of Queen's County, (continued.)

NUMBER OF TOWNSHIPS.	No. of bushels of Turnips	No. of bushels of other Roots	Apples and other Fruit, (value) £ s. d	No. of tons of Hay	Number of bushels of Beans	Number of bushels of Peas	Number of bushels of Vetches	Number of pounds of Flax	Number of Flax Manufactories	Number of acres covered with Shell Manure	Number of acres covered with Lime	Pounds of Ollcesia manufactured during the past year	Pounds of Butter	Number of Fanning Mills	Number of Mowing Machines	Number of Stumping Machines	Number of Hay-making Machines	Number of Hay Elevators	Number of Mud Diggers	Number of other useful Machines	Number of Carts, Trucks and Truck-wagons	Number of Riding Wagons and Carriages, Wood Sleds and Jaunting Sleighs	Number of yards of Cloth manufactured during the past year (fulled)	Number of yards of Cloth manufactured during the past year (not fulled)	Number of Threshing Machines	Number of Homes
No. 49,	15965	170	178 0 0	1739	27	107		657		809	211	2416	24257	31	41	5		52	4	35	76	299	571	2167	8183	33	509
No. 50,	11612	12	112 0 0	1839	94	39		698		419	151	7406	33750	28	30		1	28	2	261	562	2075	9854	24	494
No. 57,	5294	71	74 0 0	1272	3½	19½		1506	5	146	133	4473	16600	26	23		34	6	12	481	541	4270	11143	21	560
No. 58,	1192	7	30 0 0	408				988			16	2331	9438	13	3		5	1		161	267	2076	8847	18	292
No. 60,			5 0 0	388				184			5	2095	6433								163	224	1670	5345	6	230
No. 62,	611	6	5 0 0	465	8	2		1023			3	2075	9004		5		1	2	4	115	187	1855	5615	9½	233
Total,	34674	272	404 0 0	6111	48	71		5056	5	1174	519	20796	99482	98	111	5	97	4	72	94	1480	2352	15013	43987	108½	2438

Fourth Electoral District of Queen's County, (continued.)

NUMBER OF TOWNSHIPS	Number of Neat Cattle	Number of Sheep	Number of Hogs	NATIVES OF					Number of Churches	Number of Schoolhouses	Number of Brewing and Distilling Establishments	Number of Tanneries	Pounds of Leather manufactured during the past year	Pounds of Tobacco manufactured during the past year	No. of Fishing Establishments	No. of barrels of Mackerel cured during the past year	No. of barrels of Herring or Alewives	Quintals of Codfish or Hake	No. of Boats owned for fishing purposes	Gallons of Fish Oil made during the past year	No. of men engaged in Fishing	No. of Fish Barrels manufactured during the past year	No. of Coopers' Shops	Pounds of Hake Sounds cured during the past year	Value of Preserved Shell and other Fish prepared during the past year	No. of Salmon taken during the past year, and the value thereof
				England	Scotland	Ireland	British Provinces	P. E. Island	Other Countries																	
No. 49,	1242	3054	903	14	19	96	30	1480	13	5	6			1	4000				36	110		9	6			
No. 50,	1430	3875	085	25	61	32	31	1358	4	5	7								17	104	15	9	8	11	21	
No. 57,	1508	4571	1470	7	205	62	29	1630	1	4	7			2	600				1	445	12	13	4	3		
No. 58,	829	2263	478	4	133	49	32	1040		2	6			1	20					278	55	18	10			
No. 00,	651	1680	358		186		28	747			7								½	139	31½	6	38½	12		
No. 62,	753	1762	432	4	113	2	18	815	2	5				3	1719				3	6	436	33½	36	184	51	
Total,	6503	17205	4615	54	717	241	177	7070	18	18	38			7	6339				3	60½	1512	447½	91	244½	83	

Fourth Electoral District of Queen's County, (concluded.)

NUMBER OF TOWNSHIPS	No. of Grist Mills	Mills, whether driven by steam, water or horse power.				No. of Steam Engines, for mechanical or other purposes	No. of Lime Kilns	Barrels of Lime manufactured during the past year	No. of Brick Kilns	No. of Bricks manufactured during the past year	No. of Carriages and Sleighs manufactured during the past year	Yards of Cloth manufactured during the past year	No. of Cloth Factories	No. of Sewing Machines	No. of Pianos, Melodeons and Organs	GENERAL REMARKS.
		No. of Carding Mills	No. of Saw Mills	No. of Fulling and Dressing Mills	No. of Shingle and Lath Mills											
No. 49,	3		6	1			2							9	4	
No. 50,	1	1	3		3		5	1720	1	2500	5			7	1	
No. 57,	5	1	4		3		3	1100			31	15413		12	3	
No. 58,	3	1	3	1	4		3	600				12000		4	1	
No. 60,	1		3		1						11	6694		1		
No. 62,	3	2	2	1			1		1					1		
Total,	16	5	21	3	11		11	3120	2	2500	66	34107		34	9	

City of Charlottetown and Royalty.

| No. of families | MALES | | | | | | FEMALES | | | | | | Deaf and dumb | Blind | No. not vaccinated nor had Small Pox | Total number, including servants and apprentices | No. of married persons | No. of single persons | No. of issue | Married during the past year | Deaths during the past year | Births during the past year | INDIANS | | Members of the Church of England | Presbyterian Church of the Lower Provinces | Kirk of Scotland | Roman Catholics | Methodists | Baptists |
	Under 5 years	From 5 to 16	From 16 to 21	From 21 to 45	From 45 to 60	Upwards of 60	Under 5 years	From 5 to 16	From 16 to 21	From 21 to 45	From 45 to 60	Upwards of 60											Males	Females						
1520	558	1109	610	1176	470	225	584	1103	697	1511	482	192	2		2069	8807	2301	6500	53	58	134	205			1507	499	1103	3826	1791	256

City of Charlottetown and Royalty, (continued.)

Bible Christians	Quakers	Universalist	Other Denominations	No. of acres held in fee simple	No. of acres held by lease, or agreement for lease	No. of acres held by verbal agreement	No. of acres held, as occupants, being neither freeholders nor leaseholders	No. of persons holding land of First quality	Second quality	Third quality	No. of acres of arable land	No. of bushels of Wheat	No. of bushels of Winter Wheat	No. of bushels of Barley	No. of bushels of Oats	No. of bushels of Buckwheat	No. of bus. of Indian Corn	No. of bushels of Clover Seed	No. of bushels of Timothy Seed	No. of bushels Potatoes	No. of bushels of Turnips	No. of bushels of other Roots	Apples and other Fruit, (value) £ s. d	No. of tons of Hay	Number of bushels of Beans	Number of bushels of Peas
272	1	5	45	3800	65	6		51	16	9	5532	1943	859	6469	28098	323		3	70	27092	56378	1183	90 0 0	1602	5	

City of Charlottetown and Royalty, (continued.)

Number of bushels of Vetches	Number of pounds of Flax	Number of Flax Manufactories	Number of acres covered with Shell Manure	Number of acres covered with Lime	Pounds of Cheese manufactured during the past year	Pounds of Butter	Number of Fanning Mills	Number of Mowing Machines	Number of Stumping Machines	Number of Hay-making Machines	Number of Hay Elevators	Number of Mud Diggers	Number of other useful Machines	Number of Carts, Trucks and Truck-wagons	Number of Riding Wagons and Carriages, Wood Sleds and Jaunting Sleighs	Number of yards of Cloth manufactured during the past year (fulled)	Number of yards of Cloth manufactured during the past year (not fulled)	Number of Threshing Machines	Number of Horses	Number of Neat Cattle	Number of Sheep	Number of Hogs	NATIVES OF						Number of Schoolhouses	Number of Churches	Number of Brewing and Distilling Establishments
																							England	Scotland	Ireland	British Provinces	P. E. Island	Other Countries			
3	446	1022	405	12270	25	29	2	12	7	21	244	348	604	230	305	16	630	842	768	921	410	246	656	745	6507	153	9	10	5

City of Charlottetown and Royalty, (concluded.)

Number of Tanneries	Pounds of Leather manufactured during the past year	Pounds of Tobacco manufactured during the past year	No. of Fishing Establishments	No. of barrels of Mackerel cured during the past year	No. of barrels of Herring or Alewives	Quintals of Codfish or Hake	No. of Boats owned for fishing purposes	Gallons of Fish Oil made during the past year	No. of men engaged in Fishing	No. of Fish Barrels manufactured during the past year	No. of Coopers' Shops	Pounds of Hake Sounds cured during the past year	Value of Preserved Shell and other Fish prepared during the past year	No. of Salmon taken during the past year, and the value thereof	Mills, whether driven by steam, water or horse power.				No. of Steam Engines, for mechanical or other purposes	No. of Lime Kilns	Barrels of Lime manufactured during the past year	No. of Brick Kilns	No. of Bricks manufactured during the past year	No. of Carriages and Sleighs manufactured during the past year	Yards of Cloth manufactured during the past year	No. of Cloth Factories	No. of Sewing Machines	No. of Pianos, Melodeons and Organs
															No. of Grist Mills	No. of Carding Mills	No. of Saw Mills	No. of Fulling and Dressing Mills	No. of Shingle and Lath Mills									
12	137800	61892	5	2250	400	750	20		760	247	5500	6	150	£1400 £100	3	1		1	8	10	23000		358				300	309

First Electoral District of King's County.

NUMBER OF TOWNSHIPS	No. of families	MALES.						FEMALES.						Deaf and dumb	Blind	No. not vaccinated nor had Small Pox	Total number, including servants and apprentices	No. of married persons	No. of single persons	No. of insane	Married during the past year	Deaths during the past year	Births during the past year	INDIANS.		Members of the Church of England	Presbyterian Church of the Lower Provinces
		Under 5 years	From 5 to 16	From 16 to 21	From 21 to 45	From 45 to 60	Upwards of 60	Under 5 years	From 5 to 16	From 16 to 21	From 21 to 45	From 45 to 60	Upwards of 60											Males	Females		
No. 43,	183	82	134	32	152	42	31	62	100	41	152	42	38			198	917	308	609	4	8	6	16			10	300
No. 44,	200	75	158	54	143	57	41	77	137	82	141	52	42	1	2	227	1051	322	732	2	13	21	26			7	78
No. 45,	260	98	231	110	265	85	58	84	183	121	275	77	40	3		641	1622	400	1213	3	28	12	20			33	40
No. 46,	117	50	117	62	130	53	25	43	106	51	156	45	22	1		304	860	245	615		16	5	5				7
No. 47,	174	65	131	58	155	69	41	61	137	50	175	65	41	1	2	297	1057	291	763	3	21	12	18	2	2		19
Total,	964	370	760	316	845	306	191	327	672	354	899	281	183	2	8	1667	5510	1578	3982	12	86	56	89	2	2	56	444

First Electoral District of King's County, (continued)

NUMBER OF TOWNSHIPS	Kirk of Scotland	Roman Catholics	Methodists	Baptists	Bible Christians	Quakers	Universalists	Other Denominations	No. of acres held in fee simple	No. of acres held by lease, or agreement for lease	No. of acres held by verbal agreement	No. of acres held, as occupants, being neither freeholders nor householders	No. of persons holding land of First quality	Second quality	Third quality	No. of acres of arable land	No. of bushels of Wheat	No. of bushels of Winter Wheat	No. of bushels of Barley	No. of bushels of Oats	No. of bushels of Buck-wheat	No. of bus. of Indian Corn	No. of bushels of Clover Seed	No. of bushels of Timothy Seed	No. of bushels Potatoes
No. 43		551	7						6028	1198	537	3398	52	59	4	3342	1978		3683	28297	76½	11	1¼	87	46271
No. 44	18	949	2						9844	780	180	218	125	48	10	4311	2011		3807	31850	68			60	11781
No. 45		1468	20	49				12	20199	385	460	140	143	61	3	6095	2491		4121	53155	115			110	53591
No. 16	2	752		16				23	4650	3942	112	2990	43	76		2334	1064	83	1527	20820	6			17¼	20859
No. 47	2	739	2	285	1			9	14941	2153	491	160	80	76	6	5513	3825	4	4389	54069	82			104	51027
Total,	22	4502	31	410	1			44	55662	8058	1780	6912	449	320	23	21595	11369	87	17527	188197	347½	71	1¼	378½	183529

First Electoral District of King's County, (continued)

NUMBER OF TOWNSHIPS	No. of bushels of Turnips	No. of bushels of other Roots	Apples and other Fruit, (value)	No. of tons of Hay	Number of bushels of Beans	Number of bushels of Peas	Number of bushels of Vetches	Number of pounds of Flax	Number of Flax Manufactories	Number of acres covered with Shell Manure	Number of acres covered with Lime	Pounds of Cheese manufactured during the past year	Pounds of Butter	Number of Fanning Mills	Number of Mowing Machines	Number of Stumping Machines	Number of Hay-making Machines	Number of Hay Elevators	Number of Mud Diggers	Number of other useful Machines	Number of Carts, Trucks and Truck waggons	Number of Riding Waggons and Carriages, Wood Sleds and Jaunting Sleighs	Number of yards of Cloth manufactured during the past year (fulled)	Number of yards of Cloth manufactured during the past year (not fulled)	Number of Threshing Machines	Number of Horses
			£ s. d																							
No. 43,	1333	9	39 10 0	559	122½		518	82½	7½			4985	10048	10	4	1	6	9		208	300	1681	4838	10	275
No. 44,	2985	7	0 10 0	513	4 2½		1142	5½	10			2531	9961	7	2		12	1		194	298	1785	3554	4	295
No. 45,	1159			949			1616					5483	15046	24	9	1	2		3	226	412	2118	7515	24	480
No. 46,	40			193			920					2790	5105	7	1					64	150	951	3995	33	150
No. 47,	1125	22	72 16 0	939	9½ 2		1105					5524	13659	27	6		26	12 4		241	386	2127	5672	25	371
Total,	6642	38	112 16 0	3154	25½	7	5301	88	17½	2136		53819	75	22	2	46	25	5	928	1546		662	25574	96	1527

17

First Electoral District of King's County, (continued.)

NUMBER OF TOWNSHIPS	No. of neat Cattle	No. of Sheep	No. of Hogs	NATIVES OF England	NATIVES OF Scotland	NATIVES OF Ireland	NATIVES OF British Provinces	NATIVES OF P. E. Island	NATIVES OF Other Countries	No. of Churches	No. of Schoolhouses	No. of Brewing and Distilling Establishments	No. of Tanneries	Pounds of Leather manufactured during the past year	Pounds of Tobacco manufactured during the past year	No. of Fishing Establishments	No. of Barrels of Mackerel cured during the past year	No. of Barrels of Herring or Alewives	No. of Quintals of Codfish or Hake	No. of Boats owned for fishing purposes	Galls. of fish Oil made during the past year	No. of men engaged in Fishing	No. of Fish Barrels manufactured during the past year	Pounds of Hake Sounds cured during the past year	No. of Cooper's Shops	Quantity of Preserved Shell and other fish prepared during the past year and its value	No. of Salmon taken during the past year, and the value thereof
No. 43,	770	1404	882	2	8	10	22	866	9	1	3					1	161	4	201	9	104	25			24		
No. 44,	705	1008	729	4	8	39	34	965	4	3	2					3	120	24	36	21	18	7	100	1	3		
No. 45,	1275	2718	1244	5	48	33	76	1442	18	1	8					20	2120	466	2605	87	1819	31	3610	3	5887		
No. 46,	486	916	397	6	35	3	14	802		1	5					4	266		63	815	30	404	26		175		
No. 47,	1399	2455	1000	13	30	23	18	967	6	3	5			873		11	144	104	929	66	610	43		293			
Total,	4635	8501	4252	30	129	108	164	5042	37	8	23			873		39	2811	633	4586	222	3045	132	3710	4	6382		

First Electoral District of King's County, (concluded.)

NUMBER OF TOWNSHIPS	No. of Grist Mills	No. of Carding Mills	No. of Saw Mills	No. of Fulling and Dressing Mills	No. of Shingle and Lath Mills	No. of Steam Engines, for mechanical or other purposes	No. of Lime Kilns	Barrels of Lime manufactured during the past year	No. of Brick Kilns	No. of Bricks manufactured during the past year	No. of Carriages and Sleighs manufactured during the past year	Yards of Cloth manufactured during the past year	No. of Cloth Factories	No. of Sewing Machines	No. of Pianos, Melodeons and Organs	GENERAL REMARKS
No. 43,	1	1		1							10	5869		1		
No. 44,	1	1		1				1	100		10			1		
No. 45,	2	0	7		6			1	300			6180		5	5	
No. 46,	6	2	4		3							7854				
No. 47,	2	1	1		3						14			1	1	
Total,	12	4	12	2	12			2	400		34	19903		0	7	

Second Electoral District of King's County.

NUMBER OF TOWNSHIPS	No. of families	Under 5 years	From 5 to 16	From 16 to 21	From 21 to 45	From 45 to 60	Upwards of 60	Under 5 years	From 5 to 16	From 16 to 21	From 21 to 45	From 45 to 60	Upwards of 60	Deaf and dumb	Blind	No. not vaccinated nor had Small Pox	Total number, including servants and apprentices	No. of married persons	No. of single persons	No. of insane	Married during the past year	Deaths during the past year	Births during the past year	Males	Females	Members of the Church of England	Presbyterian Church of the Lower or Provinces
				MALES.						**FEMALES.**														**INDIANS.**			
No. 38,	151	69	168	56	108	51	39	64	114	80	129	48	22			471	946	251	695	2		5	14			69	244
No. 39,	127	50	124	51	99	37	30	60	114	39	124	36	18	1		433	781	189	592	3	1	2	14			3	134
No. 40,	140	69	126	54	130	44	33	67	99	53	119	43	20	3	1	433	887	256	631	2	3	2	25			46	390
No. 41,	185	79	155	52	145	71	43	75	153	53	156	62	34		1	508	1077	287	790	5	8	12	40			2	348
No. 42,	102	45	61	41	117	39	15	35	64	38	135	40	22	1		268	642	71	571	3	1		7			2	10
No. 56,	140	64	134	45	130	43	25	57	107	41	143	37	30	1		115	856	274	582		1	10	18			70	275
Total,	845	366	766	299	728	285	185	358	651	334	806	266	146	4	4	2368	5189	1328	3861	10	18		32	118		192	1401

Second Electoral District of King's County, (continued.)

NUMBER OF TOWNSHIPS	Kirk of Scotland	Roman Catholics	Methodists	Baptists	Bible Christians	Quakers	Universalists	Other Denominations	No. of acres held in fee simple	No. of acres held by lease, or agreement for lease	No. of acres held by verbal agreement	No. of acres held, as occupants, being neither freeholders nor leaseholders	No. of persons holding land of First quality	Second quality	Third quality	No. of acres of arable land	No. of bushels of Wheat	No. of bushels of Winter Wheat	No. of bushels of Barley	No. of bushels of Oats	No. of bushels of Buckwheat	No. of bus. of Indian Corn	No. of bushels of Clover Seed	No. of bushels of Timothy Seed	No. of bushels Potatoes
No. 38,		632							1	13527	988			43	94	13	3545	2261		1026	25141	210			69	33415
No. 39,	28	604	4	8						12352	820			37	64	15	3258	3446	54	907	21166	1228	31		494	22081
No. 40,	36	372	37	4					2	11424	898			30	66	40	4097	2794		2035	30882	300	112	13	62	35260
No. 41,	9	690		18	10					9925	175	1578	190	8	159	14	4052	2501		3690	33869	400	2		96	56023
No. 42,		628							2	3307	72	4800			99	3	2965	1442		2802	25905	118			33	27839
No. 56,	1	457	9	35	9					3246	1699		7490	20	58	57	3642	1359		1757	27201	98	1	1	107	58313
Total,	74	3383	50	65	19			1	5	53781	4652	6387	7689	138	540	142	21859	13803	54	12217	164214	2354	146	14	710	188531

Second Electoral District of King's County, (continued)

NUMBER OF TOWNSHIPS	No. of bushels of Turnips	No. of bushels of other Roots	Apples and other Fruit, (value) £ s. d	No. of tons of Hay	Number of bushels of Beans	Number of bushels of Peas	Number of bushels of Vetches	Number of pounds of Flax	Number of Flax Manufactories	Number of acres covered with Shell Manure	Number of acres covered with Lime	Pounds of Cheese manufactured during the past year	Pounds of Butter	Number of Fanning Mills	Number of Mowing Machines	Number of Stumping Machines	Number of Hay-making Machines	Number of Hay Elevators	Number of Mud Diggers	Number of other useful Machines	Number of Carts, Trucks and Truck-waggons	Number of Riding Waggons and Carriages, Wood Sleds and Jaunting Sleighs	Number of yards of Cloth manufactured during the past year (fulled)	Number of yards of Cloth manufactured during the past year (not fulled)	Number of Threshing Machines	Number of Horses
No. 38,	2258		6 0 0	377	6 3							1135	8106	1	2 2	1					165	256	1573	4174	36	256
No. 39,		184	18 0 0	245	12 9	7	210					1213	8382	14	6 1	2		1	5	133	244	1235	2134	11	215
No. 40,	1345	11	42 2 0	440	49 17		489			33		85a	7711	10	12 3	6		7 6	118	239	1111	3009	12	211
No. 41,	1058	20	32 0 0	396	12 5		298		4			1082	8310	5	1	1	3 11	161	280	1383	4539	9	299
No. 42,		6	1		266	1 3		609				6189	17796	11	2	1			113	131	623	164	10	219
No. 56,	4142	20	36 12 0	656	21 15	1	298			4		3578	7 38 20	14	11		2 1	123	332	1433	3365	16	238
Total,	9109	239	134 14 6	2380	104 52	8	1904		137	4		14048	60042 62	11 8	22		13 23	815	1185	7868	17385	94	1167

Second Electoral District of King's County, (continued.)

NUMBER OF TOWNSHIPS	Number of Neat Cattle	Number of Sheep	Number of Hogs	NATIVES OF				Other Countries	Number of Churches	Number of Schoolhouses	Number of Brewing and Distilling Establishments	Number of Tanneries	Pounds of Leather manufactured during the past year	Pounds of Tobacco manufactured during the past year	No. of Fishing Establishments	No. of barrels of Mackerel cured during the past year	No. of barrels of Herring or Alewives	Quintals of Codfish or Hake	No. of Boats owned for fishing purposes	Gallons of Fish Oil made during the past year	No. of men engaged in Fishing	No. of Fish Barrels manufactured during the past year	No. of Coopers Shops	Pounds of Hake Sounds cured during the past year	Value of Preserved Shell and other Fish prepared during the past year	No. of Salmon taken during the past year, and the value thereof
				England	Scotland	Ireland	British Provinces	P. E. Island																		
No. 38,	571	1500	710	7	3	42	2	884	3	1	4					21	103	4	15			150	1		£47 0	
No. 39,	591	1281	561	2	9	63	59	648		1	5			190		41	281	336	25	231	15	100		6	68 5	
No. 40,	651	1288	756	15	25	42	63	735	7	3	3					18	3½	114	3	25	14				3 0	
No. 41,	831	1625	696	8	108		22	930		1	5	1	2	2500		72		86	6	30						
No. 42,	620	1089	634	3	3	17	8	605	6	4						34	6½	43	3	20	21					
No. 56,	800	1418	683	18	19	22	29	761	12	2	2				1	685	21	216	27	70	30					
Total,	4064	8261	4100	48	172	195	183	4563	28	8	23	1	3	2750	5	877	424	790	79	376	80	250	1	6	118 5	

Second Electoral District of King's County, (concluded.)

NUMBER OF TOWNSHIPS	No. of Grist Mills	Mills, whether driven by steam, water or horse power.				No. of Steam Engines, for mechanical or other purposes	No. of Lime Kilns	Barrels of Lime manufactured during the past year	No. of Brick Kilns	No. of Bricks manufactured during the past year	No. of Carriages and Sleighs manufactured during the past year	Yards of Cloth manufactured during the past year	No. of Cloth Factories	No. of Sewing Machines	No. of Pianos, Melodeons and Organs	GENERAL REMARKS
		No. of Carding Mills	No. of Saw Mills	No. of Fulling and Dressing Mills	No. of Shingle and Lath Mills											
No. 38,	1		4		4											
No. 39,	2	2	1		1							29	4276	2		
No. 40,	2				2					1	60000				2	1
No. 41,	3		1	3	3								5938		3	
No. 42,	1		1		1	1							963			
No. 56,	2		2		4		1	100							2	1
Total,	11	3	11	1	15	1	1	100	1	60000	32	11177	2	7	2	

Third Electoral District of King's County, (continued.)

NUMBER OF TOWNSHIPS	No. of families	MALES.						FEMALES.						Deaf and dumb	Blind	No. not vaccinated nor had Small Pox	Total number, including servants and apprentices	No. of married persons	No. of single persons	No. of insane	Married during the past year	Deaths during the past year	Births during the past year	INDIANS.		Members of the Church of England	Presbyterian Church of the Lower Provinces
		Under 5 years	From 5 to 16	From 16 to 21	From 21 to 45	From 45 to 60	Upwards of 60	Under 5 years	From 5 to 16	From 16 to 21	From 21 to 45	From 45 to 60	Upwards of 60											Males	Females		
No. 51,	170	76	159	63	141	48	47	76	161	71	156	61	29	1			613	1093	278	815	3	11	15	27			10	127
No. 52,	180	79	189	50	139	52	39	63	138	51	159	51	34				502	1044	296	748		9	20	33			17	185
No. 53,	160	85	156	70	179	45	35	70	144	88	162	45	32	1	12		316	1120	309	811	1	2	10	13			82	46
No. 54,	130	62	151	41	110	47	25	68	106	55	117	46	17		2		393	845	226	619		1	8	25			26	38
No. 55,	205	130	218	81	185	67	38	103	193	89	207	53	37	4	1		482	1404	335	1069	7	6	20	48			26	303
Total,	845	432	873	319	754	259	184	380	742	354	801	256	149	6	15		2306	5506	1444	4062	11	32	73	146			161	789

Third Electoral District of King's County, (continued.)

NUMBER OF TOWNSHIPS	Kirk of Scotland	Roman Catholics	Methodists	Baptists	Bible Christians	Quakers	Universalists	Other Denominations	No. of acres held in fee simple	No. of acres held by lease, or agreement for lease	No. of acres held by verbal agreement	No. of acres held, as occupants, being neither freeholders nor leaseholders	No. of persons holding land of First quality	Second quality	Third quality	No. of acres of arable land	No. of bushels of Wheat	No. of bushels of Winter Wheat	No. of bushels of Barley	No. of bushels of Oats	No. of bushels of Buckwheat	No. of bus. of Indian Corn	No. of bushels of Clover Seed	No. of bushels of Timothy Seed	No. of bushels Potatoes
No. 51,	200	520	64	154	11			7	16058	199			116	38	10	7097	2223	21	972	53603	569		9	133	60516
No. 52,	289	349	26	130	24			24	13432	950		1105	6	145	3	5220	1658		1287	33933	719	5	9	66	54190
No. 53,	224	645	17	100					12284	701			20	115	4	4992	1329	35	1401	30853	321		3	18	44928
No. 54,	103	621	28	17	1			8	11224	44		50	25	77	40	2158	546	19	1612	17321	339			51	29850
No. 55,	70	724	72	88	25			6	20130	177	166	350	56	126	16	5717	1955		5	2651	43639	731	2		129	56445
Total,	886	2862	207	495	61			45	73128	2071	166	1505	223	501	73	25193	7711	80	7932	179439	2679	7	21	397	245929

Third Electoral District of King's County, (continued)

NUMBER OF TOWNSHIPS	PRODUCE RAISED DURING THE PAST YEAR.																						
	No. of bushels of Turnips	No. of bushels of other Roots	Apples and other Fruit (value) £ s. d	No. of tons of Hay	Number of bushels of Beans	Number of bushels of Peas	Number of bushels of Vetches	Number of pounds of Flax	Number of Flax Manufactories	Number of acres covered with Shell Manure	Number of acres covered with Lime	Pounds of Cheese manufactured during the past year	Pounds of Butter	Number of Fanning Mills	Number of Mowing Machines	Number of Stamping Machines	Number of Hay-making Machines	Number of Hay Elevators	Number of Mud Diggers	Number of other useful Machines	Number of Carts, Trucks and Track-wagons	Number of Riding Wagons and Carriages, Wool Sleds and Jaunting Sleighs	Number of yards of Cloth manufactured during the past year (fulled)	Number of yards of Cloth manufactured during the past year (not fulled)	Number of Threshing Machines	Number of Horses
No. 51,	1698	20	10 0 0	664	5 2	1196		57	93	1922	1272	22	19	5	8		10	3	189	382	2648	1745	15	333
No. 52,	2268	11	16 10 0	4784	16 6	409		99	116	2275	7250	10	4	1			10		177	152	2116	4519	10	209
No. 53,	635		1 0 0	306	7	430		237	17	808	7166	6	6	1	6		10		138	287	1876	5286	10	252
No. 54,	850	2	10 15 0	234	37	114		31		474	4491	1	1	1	2		1		76	31	971	2894	2	151
No. 55,	1428	13	22 17 0	696	28 16	743		624	8	1543	10280	11	5		12	1 12	1	235	224	2601	55339	20	349
Total,	6879	46	61 2 0	6686	86 31	2892		4864	234	7022	41915	50	35	8	28	1 43	4	815	1026	10218	69783	57	1354

Third Electoral District of King's County, (continued.)

NUMBER OF TOWNSHIPS	No. of neat Cattle	No. of Sheep	No. of Hogs	NATIVES OF England	Scotland	Ireland	British Provinces	P. E. Island	Other Countries	No. of Churches	No. of Schoolhouses	No. of Brewing and Distilling Establishments	No of Tanneries	Pounds of Leather manufactured during the past year	Pounds of Tobacco manufactured during the past year	No. of Fishing Establishments	No. of Barrels of Mackorel cured during the past year	No. of Barrels of Herring or Alewives	No. of Quintals of Codfish or Hake	No. of Boats owned for fishing purposes	Galls. of fish Oil made during the past year	No. of men engaged in Fishing	No. of Fish Barrels manufactured during the past year	No. of Cooper's Shops	Pounds of Hake Sounds cured during the past year	Quantity of Preserved Shell and other fish prepared during the past year and its value	No. of Salmon taken during the past year, and the value thereof
No. 51,	912	2282	767	4	83	117	23	864	2	2	4		1		400							6						
No. 52,	767	1683	697	14	120	17	33	854		5	5		1		4800													
No. 53,	730	640	14	59	47	104	43	866	1	6	5											12	1	0	3			
No. 54,	421	1123	356	6	75	9	29	726																				
No. 55,	985	2332	845	23	80	7	68	1217	9	4	7		1		100		6	82	159	90	30	68	16					
Total,	3821	8060	2679	106	411	254	196	4527	12	17	21		3		5300		6	82	159	108	31	74	19					

Third Electoral District of King's County, (concluded.)

NUMBER OF TOWNSHIPS.	No. of Grist Mills	No. of Carding Mills	No. of Saw Mills	No. of Fulling and Dressing Mills	No. of Shingle and Lath Mills	No. of Steam Engines, for mechanical or other purposes	No. of Lime Kilns	Barrels of Lime manufactured during the past year	No. of Brick Kilns	No. of Bricks manufactured during the past year	No. of Carriages and Sleighs manufactured during the past year	Yards of Cloth manufactured during the past year	No. of Cloth Factories	No. of Sewing Machines	No. of Pianos, Melodeons and Organs	GENERAL REMARKS.
No. 51,	1	2			2		3	300		4			1			
No. 52,	4	2	8	2	5								5	1		
No. 53,	1	1	2		1		2	100					2	1		
No. 54,	1		2		1											
No. 55,	1	1	4		6		3	362			27	9420	3	2		
Total,	8	4	18	2	15		8	762		4	27	9420	11	4		

20

Fourth Electoral District of King's County,

NUMBER OF TOWNSHIPS	No. of families	MALES.						FEMALES.						Deaf and dumb	Blind	No. not vaccinated nor had Small Pox	Total number, including servants and apprentices	No. of married persons	No. of single persons	No. of insane	Married during the past year	Deaths during the past year	Births during the past year	INDIANS.		Members of the Church of England	Presbyterian Church of the Lowor Provinces
		Under 5 years	From 5 to 16	From 16 to 21	From 21 to 45	From 45 to 60	Upwards of 60	Under 5 years	From 5 to 16	From 16 to 21	From 21 to 45	From 45 to 60	Upwards of 60											Males	Females		
No. 59, - - -	238	108	211	145	225	99	39	95	213	135	207	96	31		4	851	1604	409	1195	4	9	21	33	2	2	72	835
No. 61, - - -	207	126	200	80	144	68	39	124	178	82	164	66	27	1	1	728	1298	353	945	4	9	16	48			11	458
No. 63, - - -	164	97	157	59	132	51	29	85	145	62	142	39	31			453	1029	338	691	1	2	2	6			8	598
No. 64, - - -	137	122	235	79	180	69	60	127	191	91	215	89	35	3	1	785	1498	477	1016	1	15	14	51			56	511
No. 66, - - -	60	27	59	16	33	23	16	21	65	26	58	15	16		1	158	375	84	291	3	2	6	12				81
Total, - - -	806	480	862	379	714	310	183	452	792	396	786	305	140	4	7	2975	5709	1661	4138	13	87	59	150	2	2	147	2513

Fourth Electoral District of King's County, (continued.)

NUMBER OF TOWNSHIPS	Kirk of Scotland	Roman Catholics	Methodists	Baptists	Bible Christians	Quakers Universalists	Other Denominations	No. of acres held in fee simple	No. of acres held by lease, or agreement for lease	No. of acres held by verbal agreement	No. of acres held, as occupants, being neither freeholders nor leaseholders	No. of persons holding land of First quality	Second quality	Third quality	No. of acres of arable land	No. of bushels of Wheat	No. of bushels of Winter Wheat	No. of bushels of Barley	No. of bushels of Oats	No. of bushels of Buck wheat	No. of bus. of Indian Corn	No. of bushels of Clover Seed	No. of bushels of Timothy Seed	No. of bushels Potatoes
No. 59,	121	166	163	159	79	0		10164				71	134		6022	4112	32	1150	42263	429		13	53	60418
No. 61,	66	496	12	1	150			104	1524	9066	250	3441	6	149	51	2923	1839	29	800	33899	695 8		11	49	41108
No. 63,	221	140	18	27	17			12135	1225	657	700	1	149	6	3366	2019		1467	19684	41			12	29359
No. 64,	200	39	233	41	326			57	14364	35		29	50	100	69	6631	3971		2792	34619	812		54	107	65214
No. 66,	16	242		35				1	5707	159	9		15	32	15	2988	865		277	19931	208		2½	161	17031
Total,	624	1083	426	263	572	9	162	49894	10485	916	4170	143	564	141	21930	12806	61	6495	150396	2185	8	312	282	213150

Fourth Electoral District of King's County, (continued)

NUMBER OF TOWNSHIPS	No. of bushels of Turnips	PRODUCE RAISED DURING THE PAST YEAR.		No. of tons of Hay	Number of bushels of Beans	Number of bushels of Peas	Number of bushels of Vetches	Number of pounds of Flax	Number of Flax Manufactories	Number of acres covered with Shell Manure	Number of acres covered with Lime	Pounds of Cheese manufactured during the past year	Pounds of Butter	Number of Fanning Mills	Number of Mowing Machines	Number of Stamping Machines	Number of Hay-making Machines	Number of Hay Elevators	Number of Mud Diggers	Number of other useful Machines	Number of Carts, Trucks and Track-wagons	Number of Riding Wagons and Carriages, Wood Sleds and Jaunting Sleighs	Number of yards of Cloth manufactured during the past year (fulled)	Number of yards of Cloth manufactured during the past year (not fulled)	Number of Threshing Machines	Number of Horses
		No. of bushels of other Roots	Apples and other Fruit, (value) £ s. d																							
No. 59,	3869	5 245 0 0	564 3 4	303	1	206	314	747	9077	1	10	2	1	22 10	188	361	3664	4849	14	331						
No. 61,	1832	30 9 12 0	263 13 18	96		5		863	5237	10	2	3	10	8 4	157	183	1609	5078	10	213						
No. 63,			264 1 7			2	16	2090	3186	9	4				125	114	1055	2695	6	185						
No. 64,	1478	74 32 7 0	1149 15 14½	545		91	68	763	11425	27	5			15.5 4	277	316	2140	8852	25	348						
No. 60,	976	4 5 5 0	250 5½ 1	292		2		318	4692	3	9		8	1 7	81	131	1047	2204	1	118						
Total,	8155	113 292 4 0	2490 37½ 44½	1236	1	246	398	4781	33617 14½	30	5	10		46 75	828	1135	9521	23683	56	1195						

Fourth Electoral District of King's County, (continued)

NUMBER OF TOWNSHIPS	Number of Neat Cattle	Number of Sheep	Number of Hogs	NATIVES OF England	Scotland	Ireland	British Provinces	P. E. Island	Other Countries	Number of Churches	Number of Schoolhouses	Number of Brewing and Distilling Establishments	Number of Tanneries	Pounds of Leather manufactured during the past year	Pounds of Tobacco manufactured during the past year	No. of Fishing Establishments	No. of barrels of Mackerel cured during the past year	No. of barrels of Herring or Alewives	Quintals of Codfish or Hake	No. of Boats owned for fishing purposes	Gallons of Fish Oil made during the past year	No. of men engaged in Fishing	No. of Fish barrels manufactured during the past year	No. of Coopers' Shops	Pounds of Hake Sounds cured during the past year	Quantity of Preserved Shell and other Fish prepared during the past year	No. of Salmon taken during the past year, and the value thereof
No. 59,	960	2505	590	18	251	7	73	1243	12	1	6					2	23	16	90	4	80	8	30		30		lbs.
No. 61,	646	1761	469	12	144	68	44	1026	5	3	5		4	163			12	25	20	11	17		150	2			
No. 63,	632	1311	302	21	103	14	39	851	1	1	1							15	3	26					67		
No. 64,	1022	2627	645	69	96	4	89	1231	2	6	9	1				1	90	154	414	41	1618	99	210	6	1878	5000	
No. 66,	368	809	911	1	32	55	3	285	1	3				22			1¼	5	1	2							
Total,	3628	9013	2317	121	626	148	248	4636	21	11¼	1	4	185			3	126¼	195½	550	60	1743	107	390	8	1975	5000	

Fourth Electoral District of King's County, (concluded.)

NUMBER OF TOWNSHIPS	No. of Grist Mills	Mills, whether driven by steam, water or horse power.				No. of Steam Engines, for mechanical or other purposes	No. of Lime Kilns	Barrels of Lime manufactured during the past year	No. of Brick Kilns	No. of Bricks manufactured during the past year	No. of Carriages and Sleighs manufactured during the past year	Yards of Cloth manufactured during the past year	No. of Cloth Factories	No. of Sewing Machines	No. of Pianos, Melodeons and Organs	GENERAL REMARKS
		No. of Carding Mills	No. of Saw Mills	No. of Fulling and Dressing Mills	No. of Shingle and Lath Mills											
No. 59,	3		5		3				12	2800		66				
No. 61,	2		5		2				1	5		3	6734		3		
No. 63,	2	1	4		3				1	100			3557		1		
No. 64,			1						3	561			7157				
No. 66,	1		1		1							9	3255				
Total,	8	1	16		9				17	3466		78	20703		4		

Georgetown, Reserved Lands and Royalty.

No. of families	MALES.						FEMALES.						Deaf and dumb	Blind	No. not vaccinated nor had Small Pox	Total number, including servants and apprentices	No. of married persons	No. of single persons	No. of insane	Married during the past year	Deaths during the past year	Births during the past year	INDIANS.		Members of the Church of England	Presbyterian Church of the Lower Provinces	Kirk of Scotland	Roman Catholics	Methodists	Baptists
	Under 5 years	From 5 to 16	From 16 to 21	From 21 to 45	From 45 to 60	Upwards of 60	Under 5 years	From 5 to 16	From 16 to 21	From 21 to 45	From 45 to 60	Upwards of 60											Males	Females						
200	69	135	67	159	50	36	58	154	83	168	48	29		1	207	1056	277	779		3	5	17			156	52	272	547	10	5

Georgetown, Reserved Lands and Royalty, (continued.)

Bible Christians	Quakers	Universalists	Other Denominations	No. of acres held in fee simple	No. of acres held by lease, or agreement for lease	No. of acres held by verbal agreement	No. of acres held, as occupants, being neither freeholders nor leaseholders	No. of persons holding land of			No. of acres of arable land	Produce raised during the past Year.											No. of tons of Hay	Number of bushels of Beans	Number of bushels of Peas	Number of bushels of Vetches	Number of pounds of Flax
								First quality	Second quality	Third quality		No. of bushels of Wheat	No. of bushels of Winter Wheat	No. of bushels of Barley	No. of bushels of Oats	No. of bushels of Buck-wheat	No. of bus. of Indian Corn	No. of bushels of Clover Seed	No. of bushels of Timothy Seed	No. of bushels Potatoes	No. of bushels of Turnips	No. of bushels of other Roots	Apples and other Fruit, (value)					
3			11	5118	20½	200		62	21	13	2195	973		460	10582	70	3	2	14	22934	1073	176	£ s. d 97 10 0	382	42½	18	60

Georgetown, Reserved Lands and Royalty, (continued.)

Number of Flax Manufactories	Number of acres covered with Shell Manure	Number of acres covered with Lime	Pounds of Cheese manufactured during the past year	Pounds of Butter	Number of Fanning Mills	Number of Mowing Machines	Number of Stumping Machines	Number of Hay-making Machines	Number of Hay Elevators	Number of Mud Diggers	Number of other useful Machines	Number of Carts, Trucks and Truck-waggons	Number of Riding Waggons and Carriages, Wood Sleds and Jaunting Sleighs	Number of yards of Cloth manufactured during the past year (fulled)	Number of yards of Cloth manufactured during the past year (not fulled)	Number of Threshing Machines	Number of Horses	Number of Neat Cattle	Number of Sheep	Number of Hogs	England	Scotland	Ireland	British Provinces	P. E. Island	Other Countries	Number of Churches	Number of Schoolhouses	Number of Brewing and Distilling Establishments	Number of Taneries	Pounds of Leather manufactured during the past year
94	20	679	4614	11	1							6	5	110	177	855	2537	4	125	300	585	248	15	44	41	179	772	5	3	2	1	2	1800

Georgetown, Reserved Lands and Royalty, (concluded.)

Pounds of Tobacco manufactured during the past year	No. of Fishing Establishments	No. of barrels of Mackerel cured during the past year	No. of barrels of Herring or Alewives	Quintals of Codfish or Hake	No. of Boats owned for fishing purposes	Gallons of Fish Oil made during the past year	No. of men engaged in Fishing	No. of Fish Barrels manufactured during the past year	No. of Coopers' Shops	Pounds of Hake Sounds cured during the past year	Quantity of Preserved Shell and other Fish prepared during the past year	No. of Salmon taken during the past year, and the value thereof	No. of Grist Mills	No. of Carding Mills	No. of Saw Mills	No. of Fulling and Dressing Mills	No. of Shingle and Lath Mills	No. of Steam Engines for mechanical or other purposes	No. of Lime Kilns	Barrels of Lime manufactured during the past year	No. of Brick Kilns	No. of Bricks manufactured during the past year	No. of Carriages and Sleighs manufactured during the past year	Yards of Cloth manufactured during the past year	No. of Cloth Factories	No. of Sewing Machines	No. of Pianos, Melodeons and Organs
7	731	136	315	20	197	67	790	3	6						1					300				3392		23	17

ABSTRACT OF GENERAL REMARKS.
APPENDED BY THE ENUMERATORS TO THE FOREGOING RETURNS.

LOT OR TOWNSHIP No. 1.
HON. STANISLAUS F. PERRY, enumerator.

The roads through Lot 1 were in a bad state at the time the Census was taken, owing a good deal to the season of the year, but, with the exception of the Palmer and Horse Head Roads, travelling is good in Summer. The bridges are without exception bad, especially the bridge over Big Tignish Pond. The market places in Lot 1 are at Hall's & Co., Tignish, and at the Hon. G. W. Howlan's, Tignish Run; but the most part of the produce of this Lot is taken to Cascumpec, a distance of fifteen miles, and some sections are twenty miles from that place. The catch of fish last year was only about half the quantity caught the year before. There are, in this Township, 1 Grammar School, 7 School-houses, 1 Convent School, 1 Roman Catholic Chapel, and 1 Episcopalian Church.

LOT OR TOWNSHIP No 2. — CHAS. McCARTHY.

The land on Lot 2 is of second quality, and the people are generally poor, caused chiefly by their great attention to fishing, and their neglect of their farms. The principal markets are Tignish and Alberton, distant from two to fifteen miles. The roads throughout the Lot are very bad, and the building of the proposed Railroad to Tignish must benefit the inhabitants exceedingly.

LOT OR TOWNSHIP No 3.—HENRY GORDON.

The land in Montrose is the only land of first quality on this Township. On the Tignish and Western Roads, and in Kildare and Mimnegash the land is of second quality, and on the Mimnegash Road it is of third quality. Shell manure, in great abundance, can be obtained near Montrose. The markets resorted to are Alberton and Campbelton, distant from four to eight miles.

LOT 4.—PATRICK CONNICK.

The land in and around Alberton is of a very poor quality. The roads are good, and the inhabitants are near to one of the very best shipping places in the County. The surplus produce of the north end is generally shipped from Alberton, at any season, with safety. Kildare River, (West) is within two and a-half miles of Alberton. The inhabitants are well-to do farmers, with good farms, near to inexhaustible beds of musselmud, raising large crops of grain and potatoes. They ship their surplus produce at Alberton, and deal principally with Messrs. Reid Bros. and the Hon. G. W. Howlan. The people of Alberton vicinity deal generally at Alberton, and dispose of their surplus produce at that place. The people of the Dock Settlement are well-to do farmers. They manure their land with shell manure, which is abundantly supplied in the beds of the rivers in the vicinity of the Dock River. They deal generally at Alberton, with the Hon. G. W. Howlan and Reid Bros. The land around Alberton is of a light nature. The farmers have labored hard in manuring it, and now they have first-class farms. The farmers of Western Road (East) have a great deal more to contend with than their more fortunate neighbors of the Dock Settlement. They had and have to apply the axe to the stout beech, to clear a place for their

ABSTRACT OF GENERAL REMARKS.

dwellings. The land is of medium qua'ity. The inhabitants, who are generally poor, dispose of their surplus produce at Alberton. The farmers of the Western Road had a great deal to contend with in clearing the forest. They came here from Canada. They have pretty large clearances for the time they have been settled here. They deal principally at Alberton. The settlers on the Clark Road are principally French Canadians, who settled there on the Government purchase. The land is very good. They are making large clearances and putting up very nice buildings. It will be one of the nicest settlements on the Township in a few years. HILLS RIVER, which is about two miles from the Clark Road, is a pretty old Settlement. Most of the farmers are in good circumstances, and near to inexhaustible beds of musselmud. They deal principally with merchants at Alberton, in surplus produce, &c. The farmers of Kildare River (East Side) are not as well-to-do as those of the West Side. The land which is very light is to a great extent covered with dwarf black spruce, and, although musselmud can be obtained near to them, they do not raise enough produce for home consumption. The Kildare Irish are in pretty good circumstances. They raise more than is consumed at home, and sell on an average about forty pounds worth of produce annually, which they dispose of at Alberton. CAMPBELTON, Lot 4, is a small village with two merchants doing a good fishing and mercantile business. It is situated in a flourishing settlement, fronting on the Straits of Northumberland. There are first-class farms all around Campbelton. The farmers raise a large quantity of surplus produce, potatoes, oats, pork, beef, &c. Campbelton, or Sturgeon's Shore, Lot 4, is first-class land. The farmers are well to-do, and raise a large quantity of surplus produce. They dispose of large quantities at Campbelton and Alberton. They deal principally at Alberton. The New Dock Road is a new settlement recently opened out from the Dock to Campbelton, Lot 4. It is principally settled with new farmers, who are cutting down the forest and making new homes. The land is not of the best quality, but when opened up properly and stumped it will be a fine level settlement.

Lot 5.—No remarks.

LOT 6.—JOHN CLARK.

Cascumpec, which is situated in this Township, is a thriving village not far from shipping, and convenient for fishing.

LOT 7.—DONALD C. RAMSAY.

The land on this Township is of good quality in general. The roads and bridges are in a poor condition. The market most resorted to by the inhabitants and merchants is New Brunswick. West Point is distant from Shediac about 25 miles, and from Richibucto about 16 miles. A wharf is much needed at West Point, to enable farmers and traders to ship produce to market. This being the only place suitable for a wharf, and being so near Shediac or Point du Chene it would be a great accommodation if completed. A lighthouse is also needed greatly there, as great numbers of vessels run for shelter to it, and as there is no way of guidance, is difficult for a stranger to make it in safety in thick weather.

LOT 8.—JOHN CURRIE,

The quality of the land on this Township is in general good, and well suited for most all kinds of farming. Some of the soil is wet, but yields. The disadvantages of this Township with regard to road and water communication are very great. There is no proper place of shipping within the Township, and the nearest market, by road, is Alberton, which is distant about 25 miles from most of the inhabitants. The market most resorted to is Summerside, on account of the difference in the prices. When West Point Wharf is completed, there will be a place of shipping convenient to all within the Lot. Messrs. A. & A. Ramsay turned out about £1000 worth of lumber from their mills last year.

LOT 9.—JOHN McDONALD, (Captain.)

About one-half of the land on this Township is good, and the remaining half is poor. The roads are average. Water communication is poor. The markets,—Alberton, Port Hill and Summerside, are distant respectively fifteen, twenty-two and thirty-five miles. The latter is most resorted to. Agriculture, the general occupation of the inhabitants, is in a backward

ABSTRACT OF GENERAL REMARKS.

condition. Several are engaged in spring herring fishing, and very few in mackerel and cod fishing. The land on this Township is all rented, except the Glebe Lot, and is owned by Miss Sullivan. The leases are for nine hundred and ninety-nine years, at one shilling per acre, nine years to full rent, commencing the third year at three pence per acre. There are only one Schoolhouse and one Chapel on Lot Nine.

Lot 10.—No remarks.
Lot 11.—No remarks.

LOT 12.—ALBERT WILLIAMS.

The land on this Township is in general good, except barrens and swamps, which extend over one-fourth of it. On the North Side the land is settled, and water communication is good, but the roads and wharf accommodation are bad. On the south side the land is more swampy, and not so much settled as the north side. Water communication and roads on this side, are bad. The markets resorted to by this Township are Bideford, Port Hill and Summerside.

LOT 13, (including Lennox Island)—W.R. ELLIS

This Township, like most of the country, is level, in some parts a little rough and hilly. The land on the whole is fertile. Some of the best farms are to be found in the vicinity of Port Hill. These farms are pretty, occupying, as many of them do, a beautiful site on Richmond Bay. Port Hill is noted for its activity in the shipbuilding business. Roads are tolerably good, and are being improved. This should be the route for the Mails to Tignish. The farmers here find a ready and convenient market for their surplus produce at the establishment of the Hon. John Yeo, who exports largely to the home market. Places of shipping are few—there is only one wharf (Mr. Yeo's) where you can conveniently ship. The public wharf (Cooper's) is in a dilapidated condition, and not at all safe for a place of shipping. The rivers and streams which are many, are famous for the abundance and excellence of their fish, and many of them still afford excellent sport in this direction. The principal species of fish in these waters are salmon, trout, herring and mackerel. There is a large business done in the oyster trade. The oyster here is proverbial for its excellence. Lot 13 has one Episcopalian Church. and one Presbyterian Church in the course of erection, and one Bible Christian Church. Has four Schools, daily average of scholars, over 30. Has, also, a Free Mason's Lodge.

Lennox Island is of sufficient beauty to attract the attention of a tourist. There is much alluvial flat along the margin of the Island. The land is very good, and produces excellent wheat, as well as barley, oats and potatoes. Lately, the inhabitants have turned their attention more to farming and stock raising than to hunting—their former avocation. Several nice houses now occupy the places where once the temporary wigwams stood. Has one Chapel (Roman Catholic), and one School, daily average of scholars, 23. This Island was lately purchased by the Aboriginal Society of London, for the *especial* benefit of the Indians.

LOT 14.—NEIL. McKINNON.

The inhabitants of the Ferry School District labor under considerable disadvantage which might be removed by closing the road now leading from the Ferry towards Port Hill, and opening the same from the cross roads in a direct line to somewhere about James L. Gillis'. The road communication is about the same as in other Townships, and appears to me to be satisfactory. The people of Lot 14, together with no small portion of the neighboring Townships, labor under serious inconvenience and loss of time for want of a wharf, especially at shipping time, when boats have to be employed for shipping produce on board of vessels. The markets most resorted to by the inhabitants are Summerside and Port Hill, the former being the principal one. A few vessels in shipping time come up Grand River to load with oats. They can easily be supplied by the farmers of the Eastern end of the Township. About two-thirds of the produce raised on this Lot is hauled to Summerside, which is distant about fourteen miles. The quality of the land is generally good. Although many farmers classed their farms as second quality, yet there are few of them that in my opinion are not first-class farms The new road lately opened from McIsaac's to Lot 15 (which might be called the Aldous Road) should be made passable for carriages as soon

ABSTRACT OF GENERAL REMARKS.

as possible, as there are about ten or twelve families lately settled there who have no carriage road in summer.

Lot 15.—JOSEPH N. GALLANT.

The land on this Township can be classed as second quality, but the vacant land and a good part of what is taken, is not fit for cultivation, being either low and swampy or barren. That which is fit for cultivation is well adapted for hay and oats. The nearest and almost only market is Summerside—being an average distance of about fifteen miles. The roads are almost impassable in the spring and autumn, which makes it very difficult for farmers to take their produce to market. There is a harbor with sufficient depth of water to admit loaded vessels of from thirty to forty tons. A wharf is in construction, and when finished, will greatly facilitate the transportation of produce, and add materially to the trade of the place. There is a new vessel suitable for the harbor, and some large boats owned here. The herring fishing is generally good in the spring, but as a fishing place for mackerel, it is only second rate.

Lot 16.—No remarks.

Lot 17.

The land in general on this Township is of good quality. It is well supplied with roads, which are kept in very poor repair. There are eight vessels building at Summerside. There are three schoolhouses, viz: two district schools and one grammar school, at Summerside.

Lot 18, and Princetown and Royalty.
ARCHIBALD McGOUGAN.

A part of the land in this Lot is in very good condition and well cultivated, but a portion of it—the Misses Stewart's estate—is very poor, being far from shell manure, and most of the farmers on it have small farms of about 50 acres. The principal market is Summerside, but a large quantity of oats is sold in Malpeque. The roads are very bad.

Princetown and Royalty. — The principal market for Oats, is England. Barley and Pork are disposed of principally at Summerside.

Potatoes and Turnips—I may say, none are shipped. Wharf accommodation is poor; vessels drawing nine feet of water, cannot finish loading along-side. The land, in general, is pretty good; farmers have raised good crops hay since they commenced using mud. Roads very bad.

Lot 19.—DAVID WALKER.

The quality of Land on this Township is good, and that portion thereof not held in fee simple, is nearly all taken up and held under lease for 999 years. The public roads are tolerably good in the summer season, but very bad in the spring and fall of the year. Summerside affords a good and convenient market for all the surplus productions of this Town-hip, and is distant from the nearest point, two miles, and from the farthest point, about twelve miles.

Lot 20.—RICHARD READY.

The soil on this Lot is of a dry and sandy nature, and requires considerable manuring to make it yield heavy crops. The land in general may be classed as second quality, but some of it is poor and rocky, on the south side of the South west River. Several of the farms in the centre contain a great quantity of red sandstone, which renders them unfit for cultivation. On Graham's Road, a considerable quantity of sandstone is also found, and in a less extent in Long River. This Lot is intersected by the South-west River, which has become a source of wealth to many farmers, on account of the large quantities of shell manure taken from it during these last few years. No toil or expense has been spared by the farmers in trying to improve their farms. In the settlement of Irishtown, vast quantities of limestone of excellent quality exist. Two kilns are in course of construction and they will be in operation this spring. An experienced farmer, Mr. Geo. Mallet, informed me that he had used the lime made from imported stone and that made from Island stone, and found that the latter was equally as good as the former. The surplus produce is shipped at Summerside, distant from 14 to 18 miles; Malpeque, distant from 4 to 8 miles; Long River wharf, distant from 1 to 4 miles; and Clifton, distant from 1 to 4 miles.

ABSTRACT OF GENERAL REMARKS.

The principal part is shipped at Summerside, because the prices are higher there, and because large vessels cannot go out of New London harbor. This Township is, I consider, pretty well supplied with roads; but one is yet required from the New London Road to the river on the north side, some place between James E. Warren's and Willia n Painter's, as there is no way of people getting to the river to haul mussel-mud, except through private property. Most of the farmers on the Lot are comfortably situated, the result of much toil, perseverance and industry.

Lot 21.—GEORGE McKAY.

Clifton is under great disadvantages for the want of a Mail to connect with Summerside. Under present arrangements the Mails from Summerside are carried round by Charlottetown and Rustico. If a sum sufficient to carry the Summerside and Charlottetown Mails to Campbelton Office, a distance of seven miles, could be obtained, it would be a great benefit to the settlement in general, and business men in particular.

Trout River Settlement is under great disadvantages for want of a road to Mill Vale Mills, as they have none except a track over hills, which cannot be made passable. But if the Government would purchase a right of-way of road for about 25 chains they are willing to make the road at their own expense. High tides in Autumn destroy the Causeway across the marsh, near Stanley Bridge.

Lot 22.—EDMUND CRABB.

The land in general on this Township is of second quality. The principal markets are Charlottetown and Stanley Bridge, distant from 2 to 18 miles.

Lot 23.—JOHN McDONALD.

New Glasgow is a good farming settlement, and the people are in comfortable circumstances. Most of the people on the Cavendish Road are French and very poor. Cavendish is one of the best farming settlements on the Island, and the people are very comfortable. This Township is almost altogether fit for cultivation. The minority on it are comfortable : the majority are more than comfortable. Upon the whole, there is a decided improvement made in every respect on this Township, since the census was last taken.

Lot 24.—No remarks.
Lot 25.—No remarks.
Lot 26.—No remarks.
Lot 27.—No remarks.
Lot 28.—No remarks.

Lot 29.—NEIL McKINNON.

DeSable.—The land is very hilly. A large quantity of sea weed comes in on the shore, but as there is no public road leading to the shore, some of the farmers are unable to get any of it. Mussel Mud distant about five miles.

Melville Road.—The land very hilly. People very industrious. They have made quite a progress in buildings, &c. They cannot raise much hay, not having commenced to use lime for their lands.

Crapaud.—Plenty of seaweed and mussel mud close at hand. The land in general is in a good state of cultivation, and the soil is good.

Victoria is a small village on the Northern side of Crapaud Harbor, where considerable traffic has been carried on during the last few years. It contains about 130 inhabitants, and is the shipping place for Tryon (South), part of Lot 67 and Lot 30.

The Old Tryon Road is very hilly. Many farms along it are nearly exhausted for want of manures, and the soil in many places is light and stony.

Lot 30.—ARCH'D. C. McNEILL.

The Appin Road is in a bad state, being full of high hills, &c., and the people are far from market. A road in the New Back Settlement is very much required. The inhabitants cannot get to market or any other place without going through their neighbour's farms. They have about two miles to go before they can get to the public road, and are about five miles from the nearest market.

Lot 31.—AUBREY FOWLE.

The land is good. The distance from Charlottetown is from nine to twelve miles.

ABSTRACT OF GENERAL REMARKS.

Lot 32.—CHARLES HOOPER.

The soil is of a medium quality; nevertheless it is well adapted for agricultural pursuits Fronting on the West River, and having the North River running through the centre of the Township, there is a considerable quantity of sea manure and shell mud within the reach of most of the inhabitants, which they and those of the adjoining Township have, for the last five years, taken advantage of. Wheat is not much cultivated in the Northern portion of the Township. Potatoes, Barley, Oats, Turnips and Hay, grow well, and will compete with almost any other Township on the Island. A large quantity of produce is shipped at Poplar Island Bridge ; average distance from the Southern and Western sections of the Township about 2½ miles Charlottetown is the principal market for the Northern section of the Township; average distance about 6 miles.

LOT 33.—No remarks.
LOT 34.—No remarks.

LOT 35.—JOHN A. McDONALD.

Hickey's Wharf is the market place on the south side of Hillsborough river. There is a wharf on the west side of Johnston's river, at a place called Callaghan's Point, which requires to be extended two blocks to afford a convenient place for shipping. On the north side of Hillsborough river, Apple-tree Wharf is the shipping place. The roads leading to and from these wharves, are in a very bad state, and cause much trouble and hardship to the inhabitants.

LOT 36.—JAMES E. KELLY.

Commencing at the extreme south of Lot 36, on Monaghan Road, and coming north until Fort Augustus is met. * * * *
The people in this part hold their farms on lease, at about £4 8s 10d per 100 acres, in consequence of the land being considered of an indifferent quality; yet, taking all things into consideration, they have, in general, made more progress in life than those of their neighbors who had more promising farms. In the column marked "number of years of term of lease expired," I have thought it useless to notice such, as 999 years means for ever, to all intents and purposes; therefore, to notice the like would be a mere absurdity. Some land is swampy, but good for pasture. Here is a man who made out a respectable living for himself and family on fifty acres. Here resides a very great miser—very unwilling to give statistics. I verily believe he had over 6 0 bushels of Oats; he, however, gave in but 300 bushels.
* * * *
There are others located in the central part of the Monaghan Settlement, within about two and a half or three miles of the best shipping wharfs on the Island, viz: Hickey's and Cranberry, and about sixteen miles from Charlottetown by road or river. The people of this settlement were about the first to give an example to the I land as to what could be accomplished by industry and perseverance. The Fort Augustus farms are first-class land, possessed of rare advantages, being contiguous to carding, saw, and grist mills, and about a mile and a quarter from Cranberry wharf. Lying towards the south-western part of Lot 36, is a very poor settlement—the land is very light and sandy. It has been called "Scrabble," some twenty years ago—a name indicating hard times.

Sandhill Road, East of Tracadie Bay.—You can have no conception of the misery of the place, unless you were an eye witness. They are all the unfortunate victims of Landlordism in its worst forms. Old men have been born here, and have seen their great grand children, and yet, instead of a comfortable home to keep out the rain and sleet, nothing is seen but miserable hovels. In this vicinity, the people having bad land, never made up their minds to go into farming, as a matter of industry; a great deal of precious time has been spent in fishing, by these parties, to the great injury of their farms and their own interests. Sea manure of all kinds can be procured here in abundance, and yet the people are comparatively destitute, as compared with other inhabitants of the Island elsewhere.

LOT 37.—JOHN A. McDONALD, jun.

In Point De Roche, farming is very much neglected, and although the inhabitants are bordering on the sea shore, they do not prose-

ABSTRACT OF GENERAL REMARKS.

cute the fisheries to any great extent. The land is of an inferior quality. The market most resorted to is Mount Stewart Bridge. Pisquid New Bridge would be a very convenient shipping place for the majority on this Township, if a small sum of money was expended in dredging the river.

Lot 38.—No remarks.
Lot 39.—No remarks.

LOT 40.—JOSEPH MCVARISH.

The land in this Township is in general of good quality. The disadvantages of shipping in the fall and spring are great, in consequence of the reluctance of vessel owners to come into St. Peter's Bay, owing to the bleak stormy weather of Autumn, and to the shallowness of the water on St. Peter's Harbor Bar. The great majority of the inhabitants are therefore compelled to haul their surplus produce to Mount Stewart Bridge, Cardigan Bridge and Grand River, a distance of about thirteen miles, through roads which are, late in autumn, almost impassable. The back roads leading from the Main Post Road are very much cut up, which renders heavy hauling very difficult If St Peter's Harbor Breakwater was completed, I believe the inhabitants of this Township would be greatly benefitted, as the most distant inhabitants on the Township would not have more than four and a half miles to haul their surplus produce.

LOT 41.—MARTIN MCINNIS.

The land on this Township is of second and third quality, of a sandy nature and easily cultivated, and, with the exception of about one-twentieth part which is composed of barren and swampy land, answers well for the growth of grain and root crops. The Township has every advantage as regards roads, and although St Peter's Bay extends through the centre, water communication is poor, owing to its being situated on the North side, and to the shallowness of the water on the bar. About one-half of the surplus oats is shipped at Cardigan Bridge and Georgetown, and the remainder, with surplus potatoes, &c , is shipped at the Head of St Peter's Bay. Cardigan Bridge is distant about twelve miles, and Georgetown about twenty miles, from the centre of the Township.

Lot 42.—No remarks.

LOT 43.—RICHARD KEEFE.

Nearest Shipping place—Rollo Bay. Nearest Market—Souris.

LOT 44.—MALCOLM LESLIE.

The soil of the Southern part of the Township is in general heavy. That part of the Township known as the Head of Souris is hilly, and presents a diversified appearance. The soil on the North end of the Lot is light. This Township extends across the Island. It is divided from Lot 43 by a road called the Bear River Line Road, which is much used in the fall in transporting the surplus produce from the North side of the Township to Souris Harbor. A new road, called the New Zealand Road, is partly opened from the North side to the Head of Souris; the line of it is nearly level, and if made fit for traffic, it would be advantageous, not only to the people of this Township, but also to the inhabitants of part of Lot 45. The Main Post Road across the South side of the Township, from Rollo Bay to Souris, is deeply rutted in the fall The principal part of the produce is shipped at Souris Harbor. That harbor has been much improved by the breakwater built at the East side of the channel.

Lot 45.—No remarks.
Lot 46.—No remarks.

LOT 47—JOHN BEATON.

The inhabitants on the South side of East Point to the Western part of the Lot, have a poor chance of getting to the sea shore for manure, or to ship their produce, on account of the South Lake. A considerable quantity of the land on the South side of East Point is swampy, &c. Mud is of little use as manure on this Township. Perhaps it is not properly used. Those who tried it have given it up, having found that it injured their land. The land along the North side is principally of first quality, but the difficulty of shipping produce is great, on account of bad, hilly roads on the front, and South Lake. The land about the West River is generally of first quality. The inhabitants of the Township are of opinion that if a breakwater

ABSTRACT OF GENERAL REMARKS.

was built in Campbell's Cove they would be greatly benefitted thereby. Souris is the principal market resorted to. The inhabitants on the North Side of the North Lake have bad roads, and difficulty in getting to market. The land in general is swampy, and covered with soft wood. The most of the inhabitants on the South side of the North Lake are badly off for a good road to the shore, for procuring kelp and shipping their surplus produce. They have a kind of bridge across the outlet of the Lake, but it is generally broken, the people, for want of means, not being able to keep it in such repair as would make it resist the storms and floods. East Lake is about fifteen miles from Souris, whither most of the people resort to dispose of their surplus produce, &c., although the road is very hilly, besides being bad in Spring and Autumn. A great part of the land from Black Point to East Point is very swampy, and of third quality.

Lot 48.—No remarks.

Lot 49.—Thos. W. Beers.

About one-third of the land is of second and third quality; the remainder of first quality. Pownal Bay Wharf and Squaw Bay Wharf are the Shipping places for the Western end of the Township, and Vernon River Bridge for the Eastern end. The inhabitants of the East end have a long distance to haul their produce to market, compared with those of the West end.

Lot 50.—No remarks.

Lot 51.—James McDonald.

Two-thirds of the land is of first quality, the remainder of second and third quality. There is no shipping place on the Township. Most of the surplus produce is hauled to Cardigan and Montague Bridges, and some to Mount Stewart and Brudenell. The North part of the Lot is distant from eight to ten miles from the nearest of the above named shipping places. The middle and Southern portion is from two to four miles from Montague Bridge and Brudenell. This Township seems to be well provided with roads, it being crossed by six, including the Main Post Road, between Charlottetown and Georgetown. It is divided lengthways through the centre by Baldwin's Road, running north, and Union Road, south, from the Main Post Road.

Lot 52.—William Alley.

The land is generally of second quality. The roads in the northern part of the Township are anything but good. In the Morell and Peake's Road Settlements they are very bad. A bridge on the south branch of the Morell River is much required, and would be a great advantage to both Settlements—the distance between them in a direct line being only fifty-five chains, and that by the only public road is five miles. The nearest markets, and those most resorted to, are Cardigan Bridge and Georgetown, the former being seven miles, and the latter twelve. The other Settlements are well situated as to roads and shipping places.

Lot 53.—No remarks.

Lot 54.—Hugh A. McPhee.

Part of the land is dry and very fertile, and parts are swampy and unfit for cultivation. The inhabitants of the southern end of the Township, viz., Cardigan and De Gros Marsh, ship their produce at Cardigan Wharf, and buy their goods chiefly in Georgetown. Those of Grand River, which is about the middle of the Township, ship their produce at Chaple Wharf and Cardigan Wharf, and those of Dundas and vicinity, ship theirs at Bridgetown, Dundas.

Lot 55 and Boughton Island.
Ronald McCormack.

South side De Gros Marsh —Good land in this part of Lot 55. Shipping place, Launching Wharf and Cardigan Wharf, distant about two miles. Bridgetown, a thriving place, has a wharf called Clay's Wharf. It, however, is not sufficient to accommodate the number of vessels that arrive in the fall for produce. The quality of the land in the Township is in general about second quality.

Lot 56.—Allan McDonald.

Is bounded on the west by Lot 55, on the north by Lot 42, on the east by Lot 43, and on the southern part by the sea shore, which rea-

ABSTRACT OF GENERAL REMARKS.

ders it very pleasant and salubrious. The only shipping place of any importance is Annandale. It is the market most resorted to by the inhabitants of this and the adjacent Townships.

LOT 57.—JAMES NICHOLSON.
Shipping place, Montague Bridge.

LOT 58.—DONALD R. MCDONALD.
The land in general is dry and flinty. Shipping places, Pinette and Montague Bridges.

LOT 59.—ALEX. MCLEOD.
The land is dry and sandy. The Lot lies along the Montague River. The west end of it is six miles from Montague Bridge, the nearest shipping place. Aitken's Wharf is the shipping place of the east end, distant about three miles

LOT 60.—RODK. K McKENZIE.
Melville. — Shipping place, East Pinette Bridge, distant 3 miles. Land—poor, sandy soil. Culloden—The land is rather better than that of Melville. Murray Harbor Road—Light soil and rather sandy. Caledonia—Very sandy soil and poor in general. Shipping place, Montague Bridge.

LOT 61 AND PANMURE ISLAND.
GEORGE HICKEN.

The western portion of this Township is of a light sandy nature. The soil in many parts is composed of pebbly flint stones. A great many of the inhabitants on this Lot are squatters who are very poor. Their houses are bad, and although they have schoolhouses, their education is very deficient. They are distant from Montague Bridge from 5 to 7 miles, the nearest shipping place. The east end has only one small wharf, at St. Mary's Bay, which is too small to accommodate that part of the country.

LOT 62.—DOUGALD MCDONALD
The land in general is of a light sandy nature, which is easily exhausted, especially the northern part of the Township. The markets most resorted to are Pinette and Murray Harbor, distant about twelve miles.

LOT 63.—ANDREW MILLAR.
The land, like that of Lot 62, is of a light sandy nature. This Township is well provided with roads and market places. Markets mostly resorted to are North Wharf, Murray Harbor and Burnt Point Wharf. These two shipping places are on the Lot.

LOT 64.—HENRY BREHAUT.
Quality of land, medium.

LOT 65 AND ST. PETER'S ISLAND.
EWEN MCMILLAN.

The land is in general of first quality. The water communication is excellent, but the regular boat plying between Rocky Point and Charlottetown is deemed insufficient to meet the growing wants of the inhabitants. The prevailing cry is, "Regular Steam Navigation on the Elliot or West River, between Charlottetown and Rocky Point, calling at the intermediate wharfs." Produce disposed of at Charlottetown and at the different wharves along the river. Owing to the isolated position of a portion of the Township, and the want of adequate communication by water, the distance to market is considerable.

LOT 66.—JAMES J. O'REILLY.
Head of Montague is the name of a settlement on the South side of Montague River. The farms run nearly 1½ mile from the base line of the Lot, and the houses are built within a range of from 20 to 25 chains of the stream which bounds the farms on the North side. A road runs parallel with the stream East and West across the Lot, and between the houses and the stream. The land is apparently of a superior quality. There is probably less than a third of the whole block cleared, the remainder towards Douse's Road, on the South, is covered with a good growth of hardwood. I was informed that some good ship timber could be procured. The land does not appear to be carefully tilled, and the outhouses, &c., with a few exceptions, have an untidy appearance. The stream alluded to affords very fine water power for mills.

Head of Montague (North side).—There is a remarkable difference between the quality of

ABSTRACT OF GENERAL REMARKS.

the land on this side and that on the South side. There is only one comfortable farmer on this side (Donald Gillis). The moiety towards the river is hilly, stoney and otherwise very inferior. The settlers say they cannot raise wheat on it, and the hay crop is surprisingly small. Another road runs parallel with the stream through this section. The schoolhouse is fairly located; it is near the mill, almost between the Eastern extremities of the two roads referred to, on the line of Lots 66 and 51.

The farms on Sparrow's Road Settlement are nearly all cleared of every kind of timber, but the settlers are not thriving—only a few comfortable families in the section. Tillage system very inferior, and manure making, if possible, worse. Every facility is afforded for making composts, from the quantity of fine mud accessible. Houses very comfortless, and yet some of the land is superior in quality. The road through the Settlement has lately been straightened in part, but it is in a miserable condition.

Summerville, on the Georgetown Road, is a flourishing Settlement. The people are mostly comfortable and very industrious, to my knowledge, but I have my doubts as to the successful application of their labor. Not one of them owns, or appears to know how to make a compost heap, although the materials are at hand on almost every farm. The repeated failure of their turnip crops argues strongly on this point.

At the distance of about 1½ mile from Summerville, the Settlement of Elliot Vale commences. The road runs through the farms. They are about a mile long, each: that is the width of the Lot. Most of the land is inferior. Only a few of the farmers in this section are comfortable; their system is very bad. Markets resorted to are Mt. Stewart, Montague, Cardigan and Georgetown.

Lot 67.—John McLeod.

This Lot is wholly inland, and contains no land incapable of the the highest cultivation. The soil is naturally productive, yielding all kinds of agricultural produce. Strathalbyn, in the centre of the Island, is the largest and most populous Settlement, and comprises the southern part of the Township. It is situated halfway between Charlottetown and Summerside, which are its best markets. The surplus produce raised here is considerable, and lumber of a most excellent quality abounds. The greatest obstacles in the way of improvement arise from its distance from shipping places, and the want of access to lime and shell manure. The facilities anticipated from a railroad are largely in demand here, and in no part is the question more favorably entertained by the people than in Strathalbyn.

Malpeque Road comprises the northern part of the Lot, and is more accessible to the facilities above referred to, as may be seen by referring to the annexed columns, being within a short distance of New London and Mill River. Several on this road appeared unwilling to give a full return of the statistics, owing to an erroneous impression that the end in view was to impose a tax to meet the expenditure of the railroad; and many were alarmed that the line would cross their lands, which they regarded as a nuisance rather than an accommodation.

Braidalbane and Junction Roads, chiefly in the centre of the Lot, are, to some extent, recently settled. The people—many of whom are late immigrants from Scotland—are characterized by sobriety, perseverance and industry. The Township abounds with springs, and is generally well watered.

Georgetown and Royalty.—Neil Matheson.

The harbor of Georgetown is pronounced, by competent judges, to be the best on the Island, and capable of receiving the largest vessels afloat, and is open for navigation the greater part of the year. Principal business is in shipbuilding and the export of country produce. It has also an extensive and growing trade with American fishermen, and if it only had the water accommodations to which its natural advantages entitle it, it would not only give an impetus to the trade of the Town but benefit the Eastern part of the Island in general. It wants proper steam communication with the United States, to warrant parties in building establishments for inspecting, packing, and reshipping fish, to accommodate American fishermen properly. Also. bi-weekly or tri weekly steam communication with the neighboring Dominion, to enable its merchants to compete with other parts of the Island.

Charlottetown and Royalty.—No remarks.

APPENDIX.

Arlington, Lot 14, Nov. 23, 1871.

Sir;—I have the honor to acknowledge the receipt of your's of the 22d. In reply, I beg to inform you that the number of persons whose chief occupation is fishing are three. These three were absent at the time of taking the Census, hence the omission. The eight boats, with one exception, are owned by farmers, for fishing purposes, but for their own use only,— only occasionally used, and when used they are manned only by farmers, who, I did not think, should be put in the "Fishermen" column.

I remain, &c.,
NEIL McKINNON.

Ashfield, Lot 16, Nov. 29, 1871.

Sir;—In the Census returns of Lot 16, you say there are "four boats owned for fishing purposes," while the number of men is not noted in the Census Book.

The reason is, the boats were owned by farmers, and they wished to have their names entered as such; and as they were not fishermen, in the true sense of the word, I did not note them in the Census book as fishermen, but as it is necessary, you may say: two men to each boat, —eight in all.

I am, &c.,
JOHN McKINNON.

Brae, Lot 9, Dec. 1st, 1871.

Sir;—Yours of the 22d ultimo has been received. In reply—as to the number of men engaged in fishing, in this District—I take pleasure in informing you that it is two men to each of the thirteen boats engaged, amounting to twenty-six men; that is the minimum, as no boat would be manned with fewer than two men. Possibly a few boats took in a third partner, but I cannot, at present, ascertain what number, if any, has done so.

Your's, &c.,
JOHN McDONALD.

To John McNeill, &c., &c.

www.ingramcontent.com/pod-product-compliance
Lightning Source LLC
Chambersburg PA
CBHW020901160426
43192CB00007B/1018